Thank For Reading My
Book. I know you will
enjoy it

Best Wishes

Jim Coates #39

ALWAYS A YANKEE

A Pitcher's Story;
Jim Coates, He Beat the Odds
to Become an All-Star and a
World Champion

By: Douglas Williams

INFINITY
PUBLISHING.COM

ISBN 0-7414-5762-8

Editor: Susan Pongratz
Cover design: Mike O'Reilly
Photo editor: Mike O'Reilly
Proof reader: Ed Saunders
Endorsements by: Ralph Terry
                   Bobby Shantz
                   Bobby Richardson
Photographs: from the Jim Coates family collection
Trademarks and logos: property of Major League Baseball
-- Thanks to all for helping to make this project a reality

Published by:

INFI∞ITY
PUBLISHING.COM

1094 New DeHaven Street, Suite 100
West Conshohocken, PA 19428-2713
Info@buybooksontheweb.com
www.buybooksontheweb.com
Toll-free (877) BUY BOOK
Local Phone (610) 941-9999
Fax (610) 941-9959

Printed in the United States of America

Published December 2009

ACKNOWLEDGMENTS

It has been said, "Our lives are not only shaped by who and what we love, but to an equal degree by those who love us." I would try to acknowledge everyone who has loved and supported me throughout my life, but I realize that would be an impossible job. Love, support and encouragement have come to me from so many special people that I find it hard to choose where to begin and even more difficult to know where to end. I hope anyone I fail to mention here will accept my gratitude regardless and forgive me for any oversight.

Drs. T. C. Pierce and "Jigs" Tingle quickly come to mind because of the positive words they always had for me. The many encouraging notes I received from them when others were about to give up on me were like cups of water to a man in the desert. These gentlemen raised my spirits and kept me moving forward. To my current physician, Dr. Rocky Tingle, I also extend my thanks. Like his father before him, Dr. Rocky has done a lot to keep me well and on my feet. For many years, he has been a great friend in addition to being my personal physician.

I will forever be indebted to Mr. Billy Walker, Sr., for the kindness and generosity he showed to me when I was just a young boy. He claimed he saw something special in me from the very start. And today, I don't want to imagine where my path in life would have taken me had he not come along. My appreciation for all he did continues to grow stronger as time goes by.

In times of reflection, I easily see that I fell short in some ways when it came to responsibilities as the head of my family. For my children Jimmy, Janie and Mickey, I have many heartfelt misgivings for times they needed me and I wasn't there. I regret missing so many important events in each of their lives. I can see now there were many times when a father was what they needed most and I'm sorry for the times I wasn't there to be one. For the three of them, I sincerely want nothing less than the best life has to offer.

My grandchildren are like six radiant beams of sunshine in my heart: Marissa, Jamie, Aaron, Ian, Emily and Nichole; I love each of them and they are each dear to me in a special way.

For grandson Aaron (Pribanic), I will always be his number one supporter as he chases his dreams in professional baseball. I am extremely proud that he was picked by the Seattle Mariners in the third round of the 2008 amateur draft and also of the fine showing he has made so far in the Pittsburgh Pirates' system. I wish him continued success on his path to the big leagues. And just like his grandfather, I hope he will someday wear a pinstriped uniform with a big bold *NY* on the breast!

Because of my "second-time-around" wife Dot, I am also blessed with an extended family, made up of special people who have no idea how much they each mean to me. My stepdaughter Candy and step-granddaughter Rachael have warmly accepted me into their lives and they will always have a special place in mine.

Nita is someone who has remained close to me through both the good times and the bad. For the record, she is my half-sister. But to me, she has always been everything I could ever want a true sister to be. Our relationship runs deeper that just the simple commonality of having the same father. I should just drop the "half" and tell everyone she *is my sister.*

For the success I found in baseball, I need to extend my sincere appreciation not only to the fans of the big baseball cities where I played as a major leaguer, but also to the fans and supporters in the smaller rural areas as well. Without the support of the fans, the games would never have been played. In particular, I want to acknowledge my many friends and followers from the area of my home town in rural Virginia. These folks, whether they were serious fans of the game or not, sent their good wishes, attended many of my games and turned out to celebrate my return home after winning the World Series. I continue to be grateful for the many awards and gifts they gave me and also for giving me the honor of being declared "The Pride of the Northern Neck" by the leaders and dignitaries of the region.

Naturally, my teammates throughout baseball also had a huge part in determining the positive outcome of my career. I still shake my head in disbelief when I recall some of the associations that I had in the game. To have had teammates who are listed among the greatest ever to play baseball is a concept that still hasn't sunk into my head, even after all of these years. Some of the greats of baseball like Mickey Mantle, Roger Maris and Elston Howard were all teammates of mine and I have terribly missed each of them since their passings. Yet, today I still have Hall of Fame members and great luminaries from baseball such as Bobby Shantz, Whitey Ford, Ralph Terry, Yogi Berra and Bobby Richardson who are close friends of mine and more precious to me than gold.

I am thankful to each of them and to dozens of other former teammates as well for what they have added to my life.

I played the game of baseball professionally for 19 seasons with some of the most talented players in the world. I am thankful for all of it and I harbor no regrets. There isn't anything I would change about the game, my career or the events in life that have led me to where I am today. And by the way, I also thank God everyday for giving me the opportunity to be a New York Yankee! It's been great.

DEDICATION

In loving memory of Momma;
She gave me life and love. Alone, she nurtured me.
She encouraged and supported me.
She taught me how to be tough.
But she also taught me,
It is better to give than to receive.

Ilva L. Schools
September 15, 1910 - April 29, 1982

TABLE OF CONTENTS

FOREWORD

I remember very clearly the day I got my first Jim Coates baseball card. For me, it was a very cool experience on a very hot day. I was in the back seat of my father's Buick, heading home after a Sunday morning church service. I impatiently tore the yellow wrapper from a fresh new five-cent pack of 1963 Topps Baseball Bubblegum and there he was, along with the picture cards of five other big leaguers. Coates was a Yankee and it was a big deal for any kid to get a Yankee card back in those days, since the New Yorkers had been World Series Champions for two years running. In addition to the up-close photo in his Yankee garb, what grabbed my attention was Jim's bio information on the back of the card. It noted that he was a right-handed pitcher, height 6'-4", a record from the previous season of 7 wins and 6 losses. But even more, it was his hometown that caught my eye, Warsaw, Virginia. From the front seat, Dad confirmed that he was familiar with Jim's hometown and knew that it was located on Virginia's Northern Neck, only about an hour or so away from our house.

That was quite a discovery for me, a ten-year-old, finding that a pitcher for the New York Yankees lived that close by. It gave me quite a bit to think about. I pondered things like, how often he came back to his neighborhood and the possibilities of seeing him shopping in a local store or driving on the highway. Also, there were other points I conjured up about Jim that were for certain. Surely he knew Mickey and Roger personally and no doubt he was friends with Whitey and Yogi. And it was a sure bet that he had been on TV many times and earned lots of money. But, was he a nice man? Was he friendly to little boys and did he sign autographs?

Over the years my love for baseball never slumped. That is to say, by adulthood I had become even more impassioned by the game and its history. By that time I had heard a few stories and picked up some tidbits about Jim, his baseball career, his personality and his demeanor. I heard he had teammates he didn't get along with. I read there were certain batters he threw at deliberately. And as the sports memorabilia business was taking off in the 1980s, hobby show promoters often got no response from Jim when they tried to schedule him as an autograph guest. Neither did collectors who wrote letters to him asking for his signature. I suppose it was my personal conclusion that Jim probably had very little to say, enjoyed his privacy and preferred not to be bothered. There are many cases of celebrities, former athletes and entertainers who, because of some personal issue avoid any stirring up of their past. Some of them feel that in spite of what the public perceives as a time of thrills and glamour for the star, it was actually a career that was soured by disappointment or regret, a period they would just as soon not revisit. And like anyone else, they want to leave unpleasant memories where they are.

Over the past decade or so it has been very pleasant for me to spot Jim's name popping up in ads and promotions for collector shows, player reunions and charity fund-raisers. So, I jumped at the chance to go meet the former pitcher at a couple of these gatherings, thinking such opportunities may not come up again if he, in fact, wasn't comfortable with public exposure or mixing with strangers.

It was even more gratifying for me to finally meet this man and see for myself just how affable and personable he was. I found that he was quick to smile, shake hands and share a story. For each of the fans and collectors that came out, Jim did more than just sign an autograph. He added stats, dates, inscriptions and personalizations to the photos and baseballs he signed. He answered questions, posed for pictures and patiently listened to every trivial baseball tale that was recalled by his longtime fans. But still, I was undecided. *Which one of these is the real Jim Coates,* I wondered, *the guy behind the autograph table or the elusive man that kept to himself?*

It was several years later that I happened to meet up with Jim again, and for the first time, I was introduced to his wife Dot. I was signing books at a local sports collectibles store and Jim was one of several autograph guests appearing at the promotion. By spending a couple of hours together in the store that day, we got a chance to talk and get acquainted during times when the customer lines dwindled. That's when ideas of my writing Jim's biography surfaced for the first time. We traded a few thoughts and exchanged phone numbers, agreeing to discuss the matter further.

Pre-game coverage of Super Bowl XLII was just about to start when I left the Coates's home on a Sunday afternoon in February 2008. Jim and I had finished our first recorded interview session. But at that point neither of us was certain whether or not to move forward with the project. We worked for about two hours as he detailed some of the hardships of his early life. He was honest and candid about his life and made no excuses or apologies. He opened himself in a way that indicated he was willing to tell it all. His story kept me enthralled from when I first sat down on his sofa until I pressed the stop button on the recorder. Finally, we called it a day. He walked outside with me to my car, an act of good ol' country courtesy that comes naturally when folks just finished a good visit. I made note of the license plate on his old pickup truck. 61 YANK it read. "That's a great plate you got there, Jim," I remarked. "That's really something to be proud of."

"Yeah Doug, I really am. I have many things to be proud of. I've done quite a lot in my life. I've played in the all-star game and I pitched in the World Series a few times," he reflected. "Once, I was even selected to be the starting pitcher on opening day!"

"You're right, Jim," I agreed. "You had the kind of career other guys only dream about." With that, a short silence followed while Jim was deep in his thoughts.

"And you know, Doug, I was with some other teams besides New York," he added. "I spent time with Washington and I was with Cincinnati a while and with the Angels, too. But, you know what?" he pried. "I consider myself a Yankee, that's just the way it is. I'm always a Yankee!"

I made the drive back home thinking all the way about the special afternoon I had just experienced. My thoughts drifted back to another Sunday back in 1963 when I got that first Jim Coates bubblegum card. *Amazing!* I thought, summing up my visit. *Amazing!*

It's truly an unforgettable moment when you discover for yourself that a hero from your childhood turns out to be exactly the kind of man you hoped he would be.

Douglas Williams
October, 2009

CHAPTER 1

Could This Be Real?

There it stood -- the temple of the gods of baseball, "The House that Ruth Built" -- the revered battleground of so many of baseball's most historic engagements. It was Yankee Stadium! And there I was, a tall, lanky country boy from Virginia who had just been told to report there, my new place of employment. I felt about as out of place as a skunk at a prayer meeting!

Could this be real?

Sure, I had spent the past several seasons in the minor leagues, which was considered professional baseball, if you could call it that. I had even been with the Yankees for a few days on the road in Boston and Baltimore. But this was the home of the Yankees and they told me I belonged there.

Could this be real?

My first order of business was to check in with Big Pete Sheehy, the team's longtime clubhouse attendant. Pete, who came to the Yankees in 1927, was the official "keeper of the pinstripes." Over the years this man had issued uniforms to so many of the great players of this club, like Ruth, Gehrig and DiMaggio, and now Pete had a set of Yankee pinstripes ready for me!

The navy blue cap, the white wool-flannel shirt with the distinctive *NY* on the left breast and the number *52* on the back, to me it all symbolized the class and integrity of the greatest organization in sports. "I'm now part of that organization," I whispered.

Could this be real?

At my locker I got suited up. Just fastening the buttons was a thrill. Big Pete had all of my sizes in advance so everything seemed to fit just fine. I used both hands to roll the bill of my cap to give it just the right amount of bend and after a quick check of the belt loops and a final tug on the cap, I was ready to take the field.

I passed through the tunnel connecting the Yankee clubhouse to the home team dugout. I paused long enough to notice the four steps leading upward from the dugout and onto the playing field. I took those steps and there I was, peering out at the most beautiful ballpark in the world. I continued to question myself.

Could this be real?

As I took my first steps onto the grass, I was over-whelmed by all that I was seeing. Just inside the wall in deep centerfield stood the famous monument park, erected in honor of three of the greatest Yankees ever: Babe Ruth, Lou Gehrig and Miller Huggins. The white picket façade, the trademark of the stadium, encircled the roofline. And there was the short rightfield fence, which set the boundary for the portion of the bleachers formerly known as "Ruthville." It was all too much for me to take in. It actually took my breath! It was like a spiritual experience, as those last few steps took me up on the field of Waite Hoyt and Joe Sewell, of Earle Combs and Joe DiMaggio. While I tried to accept what was in front of me as reality, I quickly began to think back and reflect on all that was behind me and the steps that really brought me here.

* * *

I was being truthful when describing myself as a country boy. I am equally honest when I say I came from humble beginnings. My boyhood was one of many shortages, particularly the scarcity of money and material things. But, within me there was never any shortage of desire and determination.

I was born on August 4, 1932, in the tiny town of Farnham in Richmond County, Virginia. I was the third of three children born to Ilva and Henry Coates, Sr. My father was someone I hardly ever knew. He left us when I was just three years old. So, with Momma as the lone provider for the household, it is easy to see why life was a struggle. Looking back, I believe she did a remarkable job of keeping us together and maintaining some structure within the family. We grew up in a very rural area situated on the Northern Neck of coastal Virginia, near the mouth of the Rappahannock River. This part of the country is known for its low, flat farmland and the commercial fishing docks for the local seafood industry, so my mother had few places to turn to for employment opportunities. But she was a very determined person, a lady who was not a stranger to hard work. Perhaps some of her strong will and determination rubbed off on me. She found a job close to home working at a country store which sold mostly groceries, meats and gasoline. She worked there six days a week, getting home each evening just in time to fix supper. Times were especially hard for her back then, but they somehow managed to get even worse.

It was a dark night on a narrow, winding country road near our house that she was involved in a horrible automobile accident. She was riding in the car with her sister Zoa and brother in-law George. The sisters had just spent the evening visiting, enjoying each other's company when the short drive back home turned out to be a near tragic situation for my mother. Her injuries were such that even after a lengthy stay in the hospital, she still needed a few months of recovery with rest at home. Momma's accident brought another time of change for all of us. Me, my brother, Henry, Jr., and my sister, Grace went to stay with our mother's parents, Grandma and Grandpa Lewis. Their place was just a few miles away, and living with them was an arrangement that we went into not knowing what to expect. It was an arrangement that was supposed to be temporary in the beginning but I, being the youngest at just five years old, continued to live with Grandma for about nine years.

3

Needless to say, she played a major part in my upbringing, as I ate, slept and bathed under her roof during the most formative years of my life.

My desire to play ball was something I seemed to be aware of as far back as I can remember. I feel like I had this passion to play ball burning inside me even before I was sure the game of baseball existed. I couldn't have known about baseball, or any sport for that matter, as there was no one in the family abreast of current news outside of our community. We had no radio, television or newspapers at home, and the adults in my life were all working hard just to have the basic necessities and were far too busy to follow anything as incidental as sports. Yet for me, I was sure about my calling in life before I was old enough to start school. I wanted to be a baseball player!

Most likely it was my older brother, Henry, Jr., who answered to the nickname "Slim," who gave me the notion that playing ball was something that the big boys did. But, being determined to follow my dreams, I wasn't about to waste time waiting to grow before starting to work on the basic skills of throwing and hitting a ball. Of course, we had no baseball equipment at home, but being able to improvise was one thing we all needed to do if we were going to get anything done. When it came to playing baseball, old fashioned ingenuity was all it took to get me started.

Black walnuts were ideal. I found them to be just the right size for throwing practice. Finding a walnut tree with fallen walnuts scattered on the ground, still in their outer hulls was something special to stumble upon. I could gather them into a small pile and have enough walnuts to get me through a fairly lengthy pitching session, working my arm to increase velocity and sharpen my accuracy. I spent many hours sweating in the sticky heat while chunking those things at any target I could find, a stump, an old rusty can or a tree trunk. Anything like that would do fine. However, there was one problem with using those walnuts for my make-believe baseballs. When those outer hulls changed colors from a bright green to a smutty black, look out. The stains left from throwing those dark walnuts would be almost impossible to remove from the fingers of my right hand. Soap and water would be of no use. Sometimes it would take a week or two for those stains to finally go away.

Momma was mindful of how much of my time and energy was spent playing imaginary baseball. In her own way, she showed support and gave me encouragement for what I was doing. Her time away from her job and house-work was very short, yet she found time enough to put her ingenuity to work and come up with what would be my first-ever piece of athletic equipment: a homemade baseball! This was a real vote of confidence that I received from her. I felt like she was showing some degree of faith in me and maybe, deep down inside, she believed in what I was doing and trusted that neither of us was wasting time.

This homemade baseball was meticulously made and proved to be quite durable. To begin this project, Momma started by tightly winding long pieces of twine into a round ball. Once it was large enough, she covered it with layers of old, worn out socks that could not withstand any more mending. The layers of socks were all hand sewn and the outer cover was stitched in a way to give it the outward appearance of an actual baseball. It couldn't be compared to those commercially produced baseballs, like a Spalding or a Wilson, but it became my most precious possession, and with a few repairs from time to time, it served its purpose for a few seasons to come.

This special ball also worked nicely for my agility drill, which I conjured up to sharpen my defense. This simple, repetitive drill was done utilizing the sloping tin roof of Grandma's old, wood framed farmhouse. By standing not far from the house and tossing the baseball onto the roof, I had to be ready to catch it as it rolled down and over the edge. The roof had evenly spaced, raised ridges where the edges of each sheet of metal lapped and connected to the adjacent sheet. By striking those corrugations, the ball could do some funny tricks, bouncing and changing directions like a pinball. It taught me how to stay on my toes and trained me to shift my weight while moving from side to side to make a good play on the ball

I never became what you would call a "slugger" when it came to my hitting records, but that was not due to a lack of batting practice as a youngster. Slim and I made our own bats from the dried limbs of hardwood trees such as oak or hickory. Once we found a limb of the proper size, we would whittle and sand it to get it to the right shape, paying attention to the handle area. That section of the bat had to be the smoothest and thinnest part to assure a perfect grip.

The two of us would take our homemade equipment, our ball and bats and head for the cleared, open field not far from the house. There we would stand about two hundred feet apart. Taking turns, Slim and I would toss the ball into the air and with our best swings, drive it in the direction of the other. Ours was a competitive game, forcing each other to backtrack a few steps with each fly ball, checking to see who was hitting for the longer distance. Even though I was the younger brother, I could always compete in this rivalry and get good wood on the baseball. However, I'm very pleased that I never had to depend solely on my batting when it came to earning a living in baseball.

.   * * *

But on this day, I'm twenty-four years old, and the days of hitting and pitching in imaginary games are all distant memories. This is my first day at my new place of business, located at the corner of East 161st Street and River Avenue in The Bronx, New York. It's Yankee Stadium, the real Field of Dreams. It's Friday, September 28, 1956. In a little more than an hour we will play the visiting Boston Red Sox. We have already captured the American League championship flag for the season, making the Yankees pennant winners seven times in the past eight years. The entire team is buzzing about the upcoming World Series and speculating who our opponents will be. Brooklyn's chances look pretty good, but the Braves and Reds might have something to say about the outcome of that tight race. With just a handful of games left, we are looking for our 97th win of the season tonight to improve on what is currently the best record in the major leagues. By judging the recent performances of our starting pitcher, Don Larsen, we should have no problems. We will begin tonight's game with Hank Bauer in rightfield, Mickey Mantle starting in centerfield and Yogi Berra behind the plate! Can you believe it?

The New York Yankees....what a team! Is this one of my imaginary games?

Could this be real?

CHAPTER 2

Keep Believing!

The years I spent with Grandma and Grandpa Lewis were not easy, believe me. It was far from the ideal situation for the three of us children. But after Momma's accident, we had no other choice. Even though it was the home of our grandparents, it was never a place of family warmth as you might expect. So often we were made to feel more like orphans than grandchildren. There never seemed to be an adequate amount of anything, especially for me, my brother and my sister. Frequently, I found it best if I stayed busy. Doing the work I was told to do or even playing outside would sometimes help keep my mind off being hungry. But hunger was one thing that never seemed to go away completely.

We were fortunate to have cornbread from time to time but even that didn't come easily. One of my jobs on the farm was to pick and shell some of the corn grown there on Grandpa's land. We kept the corn which was shelled during the week and took it to a local mill on Saturdays to be stone-ground into cornmeal. So a piece of cornbread and an occasional egg was about all any of us ever had to eat in the mornings.

My school day would typically start at sunrise and there was a lot for me to do before leaving for school. Besides cutting firewood for cooking and heating, our chickens and pigs needed to be fed, along with other normal chores given to a young farm boy. These jobs had to be finished prior to taking off on a two-mile walk to school. It was two miles each way, going and coming, on dirt roads. If I was lucky, I would pass by a wild cherry tree on the way. A few handfuls of those tangy, black cherries would help hold me over until I had another piece of cornbread or a leftover biscuit at noon. Each day, rain or shine it was my daily routine and what I found to be part of growing up as a poor country boy back in those days.

As a young boy, I can't recall many things that caused me as much grief and discontentment as having to attend school. Having to sit quietly in a classroom while a teacher lectured endlessly about reading, writing or arithmetic wasn't exactly the way I wanted to spend my time, but my attendance was near perfect and I can't recall ever being tardy, as Grandma would never allow anyone to oversleep at her house. Even when colds or flu spread throughout the school, I always managed to stay relatively healthy and hardly ever missed classes. However, concentrating on my subjects -- that was a totally different story.

For six years, I attended Farnham Elementary School in a small wooden schoolhouse, which gave me the impression it was outdated even then. Each day during classes, my mind seemed to stray to thoughts about other things, mostly outdoor activities, and mostly about playing ball. I am certain there was no type of attention deficit, like so many school kids are reported to have today. My problem was this constant urge to be outside running, climbing or throwing. Class time always seemed to run far too long and recess was always way too short.

Most of the school children then, much like today, were full of energy. I certainly was no exception. While other students were working towards their goals of becoming attorneys or engineers, I was sure, even then, that the road to the future was not leading me in that direction. A few of my old friends from school moved on to become career professionals as successful lawyers, teachers or doctors and I truly admire each of them for their accomplishments in life. But I was never suited for that type of work. I don't believe I would have survived working long hours behind a desk, regardless of the salary. No matter if it were the heat of August or the cold temperatures of January, I would always prefer being outside, working with my hands. Give me the great outdoors any day.

* * *

Seventh grade was a personal milepost that I had anticipated for a long time. At thirteen years old, this would be my first year attending Lively High School and for me, this was more than just leaving grade school. Advancing to high school meant I was finally going to be eligible for the school's varsity baseball team the following season. In the spring of 1946, signing up to play baseball was the most exciting time of my life to that point. For the first time, I was about to play ball on a field with a backstop, where the bases were ninety feet apart and where there would be nine boys on each side! I had waited a long time for this. It all sounds very simple, but this was my first time belonging to an organized baseball team. Still, I had no glove or bat of my own, only a strong desire to play. Fortunately, there were enough boys who signed up to make a full team and several of them had their own equipment. By sharing what little we had, along with the help of our coach, Jack Trew, everyone was wearing a glove whenever we took the field.

I became a pitcher right from the beginning in high school. Even though I really didn't know what I was doing on the mound, I threw the ball pretty well, well enough to catch the coach's eye. In spite of problems with my control, my speed was evident from the start. Yet, there was no one around to work with me, to give me pointers or advice concerning the mechanics of pitching. Nonetheless, I was happy just getting to play with the team. After all, I was on the field competing with boys who were often four or five years older than I was. Each game, I held my own against older, more experienced players and became aware that God had blessed me with a few advantages that most of the other guys didn't seem to have -- height, quick reflexes and a tremendous right arm!

What amounted to a turning point for me in scholastic baseball occurred at the annual May Day game. May Day was a huge, outdoor, school festival held each spring to mark the ending of another school year. As part of this yearly celebration, a baseball game was scheduled, pitting the two local high school teams which finished their seasons with the best won-lost records. Lively High had been fortunate to make it to the May Day championship; our season had been a good one. In spite of being amongst the youngest players on the squad, I had managed to win more games than any of our other pitchers.

So, when Coach Trew made his decision to have one of our senior boys be our starting pitcher for the big game, an explosion of outrage erupted from the school's student body. Many Lively students who came to watch the game were shocked when they learned of the coach's choice. Their objections could be heard all around the ball field. The consensus of the crowd was "a championship game is no place to extend senior privileges." Sure, this was the final game for our senior players, but "use our best pitcher for the big game!" they demanded. But the coach was steadfast in his decision. So, as a team, we all rooted for our pitcher as well as all of the upperclassmen in the lineup. We just needed to win!

I was anxious to get into the game, while at the same time I was consciously trying to keep my own emotions in check. Students and adults together continued to voice their displeasure with Coach Trew even after the game started. While watching from the bench, I felt good knowing the popular opinion favored me, yet deep inside I knew we would need a top effort from each of our players to win the title.

But for our pitcher, it was a nightmare! It was his worst game of the entire year. He appeared to struggle with the command of his pitches from the start, causing Coach Trew to pull him from the game in the first inning. In a bleak situation in the biggest game of the year, I was brought in to pitch in relief. I had enough speed and movement on my pitches to hang in there for the remainder of the afternoon. The result was a losing cause for Lively High, as we fell so far behind at the onset. However, I managed to shut down the opposing batters, completing the game and giving our boys a chance to win, as the score became much closer before the final out was called

Through the summer that followed and even into the next school year, the rumblings continued. All around the community and at school many of the locals were still talking about our loss on May Day. It was truly a wound that was slow to heal. Even today, more than six decades later, some folks in the area still recall that game and how that baseball championship slipped away from Lively High.

Following that season, I had a couple of years of high school baseball still ahead of me, but it was my performance at that May Day game which drew the most attention to my pitching. When the following season arrived, I was called upon to be the front line pitcher for the school. Naturally, it was a role I was proud of. Even Coach Trew assured me I had earned it. I was beginning to believe in myself even more than before. Confidence, it seemed, was what I needed most. "Keep on doing what you're doing," I told myself. "Keep believing!"

I was doing all of this with what I call "raw ability," while waiting and wondering when someone would come along to provide the help I needed to develop my God-given talent. All the while, I was certain that would happen. Surely, that person was out there, somewhere. I only needed to keep believing.

By the end of the tenth grade, my fastball was really blazing. My arm seemed to be getting stronger and what I lacked in control, I was able to make up with speed. Many of the batters who faced me were intimidated by the wildness of some of my pitches and as anyone familiar with game of baseball will tell you, "a fearful batter can only be successful if he gets lucky."

But, while things were working out well on the ball-field, the marks on my report card were in a dreadful slump. For me, the entire school year had been very frustrating academically. At just sixteen years old, I felt the pressure of being in a tight spot, like the time had come for me to make a crucial decision. Certainly, now was the time for me to take a hard look at the world of reality and what lay ahead.

The job market for the folks in my area was limited, to say the least. The working men of Virginia's Northern Neck were predominately farmers, fishermen and lumbermen. Most of the young men picked up the working trades of their fathers and grandfathers. They were people from families who had owned the same land for generations, with no intentions of leaving. These were my friends, my neighbors and my family. For many of us, the world was limited to the distance you could walk or how far you could ride along with someone who had an automobile.

I was one of them, a product of my environment. My plans were no different. I wanted to stay close to home; it was all I had ever known. Furthermore, the type of work for which I was destined would require no formal education, no diploma, or no degree. School had been an uphill battle for ten years and at this point I could not see that it had any relevance to my future. So I decided to make that year my last year of school. "For now, I'll just see what happens," I told myself. And like any other young man at my age, I was facing a lot of uncertainty.

But, something good was going to come into my life. I was sure. I just had to keep believing!

High school baseball- That's me, front row, 3rd from left.

CHAPTER 3

The Chesapeake League

During the decade following World War II, baseball was thriving across the United States. Throughout the eastern half of the country, every town big enough to have a post office, a church and a barbershop seemed to have its own baseball team. This was nothing new. Prior to the war, there were semi-pro and industrial league teams competing just about everywhere east of the Mississippi River. Once Uncle Sam saw the need to call away most of America's young men for military service, a hiatus of about six years was imposed on many of those circuits.

By the late forties, a near total resumption had taken place. Major League Baseball had gotten back on track with many of its superstars such as Ted Williams, Bob Feller and Hank Greenberg returning to take back their places on the big league rosters. Post-war prosperity was allowing America to get back on its feet socially and economically. This meant inter-town rivalries were being renewed as small businesses now had a few extra dollars to put towards sponsorship of a local ball team. Our war veterans were back to work as were young men all across the country, working fulltime but having their weekends free to play baseball.

In the coastal region of Virginia, it was the Chesapeake League that brought together the semi-pro teams of the two counties nearest my home. It was a league of simple operations compared to the expensive, over-organized sports programs of today. On Saturday and Sunday afternoons throughout the summer, local teams played out a schedule which had each team square off against another of the other nine clubs twice, once at each town's home ballfield. Just about all of the players worked during the week so they could afford to pay the league's registration fee which went towards the purchase of uniforms and a few basic equipment items. This money also paid for the umpires who worked the games in crews of two. These umpiring crews drove out from Richmond each week with each man receiving fifteen dollars per game to cover his food, time and travel.

The players of the Chesapeake League were responsible for their own transportation. Each player suited up at his home and usually caught a ride with teammates to the game. For road games, which were no more than an hour's drive between towns, players car-pooled or chipped in for gas so the whole team traveled in three or four automobiles. The most trying part of traveling for those games was the ride back home. After playing on a dusty field on a hot, humid afternoon, nothing imaginable could be fouler than a car full of cramped ballplayers in need of a cold drink and a bath. Needless to say, all windows were rolled down for the entire trip!

Every player in the league participated because of his genuine passion for the game. Baseball, by far, was the most popular sport for everyone, young and old. It was a big part of life. It was a time when baseball was truly America's pastime.

The sparsely populated counties of Lancaster and Northumberland were the extent of the Chesapeake League, with five teams from each county represented. Each of these tiny communities scattered across the area had its own town team, its favorite local players, and its own ballfield laid out to specific dimensions. Each also had its own legion of dedicated rooters who attended the games, home and away, to show support for their ball club.

I must have made a positive impression on a few of the fans and players around home with my pitching record for the high school team. After leading Lively High in wins for the year and capping off the season with some gutsy pitching in the May Day game, it didn't take long for the word to spread. Throughout the county, I was gaining notoriety. There were people talking about "that tall Coates boy who just started high school, the one with an arm like a cannon!" With this new reputation, I found myself being approached by folks around the community urging me to give the Chesapeake League a try. Semi-pro baseball might be too advanced for a fellow my age, but there were even players from the Lively town team encouraging me to join them. "Your age won't make any difference," they assured me. "It will be good for you to start young; besides, good pitching is what our teams needs most!"

Oddly enough, at fourteen years old, I found myself by far, the youngest player on the Lively semipro team. All of the other guys were beyond the age of high school, with many having returned recently from military service. I can't recall any other boys my age playing in the league. None of the other high school players in the area were invited. I was so young and without a penny to my name; all I had to offer was my raw ability, my confidence and my unfailing desire.

Many of the particulars from those days are cloudy for me today. Trying my best, I can't recall who it was that put up the money for my registration fee. But I remember I was never able to scrape up money for that, nor could I contribute gas money or take a turn driving to the games. I was forced to depend on the generosity of others for almost everything.

One source of support that I will never forget, however, was a special man in the community named Billy Walker, Sr. Mr. Walker always seemed to have a strong interest in local baseball, both scholastic and semi-pro. His son, Billy, Jr., was a close friend of mine from school and his dad could often be seen attending games or lending a hand with practice drills. It was Mr. Walker whom I thank for giving me my first baseball glove. It was a spare of his which had seen its better days, but once it was restrung, I was able to make that glove last for quite a few years. To be frank, I did this out of necessity. There was no telling when I would ever be given another glove or if I could ever afford to buy one on my own. The maker of that old mitt was something I was never quite sure of since any discernible markings from the manufacturer were long gone, except for the unmistakable head of an Indian, which was branded into the dry, cracked leather of the wrist strap. I had no way of knowing how this glove was going to play such a vital role during the developmental years of my baseball career. However, it was this decrepit, old glove that I was still using after signing my first professional contract! Incidentally, it was Mr. Walker who also gave me my first pair of spikes. I received them about the time I began playing with the Lively semi-pro team. Mr. Walker was a special kind of man who was always willing to help. He was someone who definitely had a lot of high hopes for me.

My older brother, Slim, was also a pitcher for the Lively team. Being teammates only fueled the ongoing debate about which one of the Coates brothers was the better pitcher. Which one had better control? Who threw faster? Was Slim's curve better than Jim's? Which one of the brothers would make the most of his talent? These questions seemed to go on and on without answers. However, there was one point that could never be disputed.

There were a few occasions when Slim was pitching that I got behind the plate to be his battery mate. I wasn't a great catcher by any stretch of the imagination. Yet, he was pretty comfortable with me as his backstop. Somehow, I managed to catch most everything he could deliver and that was no easy job. However, my brother wanted nothing to do with returning the favor. He never wanted to be the catcher when it was my day to pitch. This was just a part of our never ending sibling rivalry, a little something that secretly brought a smile to my face. I guess my fastball was a little too hot for him to handle. So he would gladly accept another defensive position on the field rather than catch for his little brother.

Yet, as a pitching duo in the Chesapeake League, we were among the best. We Coates boys would frequently be the scheduled starters, with one of us pitching on Saturday and the other on Sunday. And a formidable pair we were! With our Lively teammates as a solid supporting cast, it was not unusual for us to win about four out of every five games and then find ourselves sitting atop the league standings.

The best catcher on that club, Bill Clark was a truly special sort of guy. He was a teammate who had baseball flowing through his veins. And now, more than sixty years later, things haven't changed much. Bill was a ballplayer with a lot of determination. He had just returned from military service to take his place on the town team and for him, playing baseball was serious business. He wasn't about to allow my fastball be anything he couldn't handle. To help guard the palm of his left hand, Bill, on occasions, would get a freshly cut piece of raw round steak from his father's grocery market and place it inside his catcher's mitt. That extra cushion of meat protected his hand from burning and bruising. "With the help of a small piece of beef steak, I could catch just about anything Jim could throw up there!" he would boast. And this is a claim he still makes today!

Playing ball, like many other things in my life, got better once I was allowed to move back in with Momma. For years she had lived in a tiny upstairs room above the store where she worked. It was hardly enough room for her, but she somehow found a way to keep Grace, my sister, there with her for a short time. The arrangement of living with our grandparents, which had never been a pleasant situation, had grown even more difficult after Grandpa's death. Besides Grandma, there were also some of my aunts and uncles living there at the old farm house. With Grandpa gone, there appeared to be an instant clamor taking place among the adults to determine who would take over as head of the house. That was not a good place to be as a child, with so many relatives scheming to be in charge of this impossible family situation.

At the same time, school had turned into a real hardship. I began high school as a seventh grader and found myself awkwardly out of my element. There was a new mix of school kids with only a few familiar faces in the class.

There was a small group that had been with me since first grade at Farnham, but some of those old friends seemed different. Many of them seemed to keep their distance from me. There were a lot of adjustments to make in high school, including lots of new students with critical, narrow minded attitudes to which I wasn't accustomed. Most of these students came from traditional families. Some had fathers who were professionals- lawyers and bankers and such. This huge social gap took me by surprise and it was a problem I wasn't prepared to solve. But I showed up for class each day with not much more than my own personal pride. Those kids in the social set had nothing to do with me. It was as if I carried the plague. I was quite a loner at the start of high school but a very determined one. I became more confident than ever and told myself I would use what I had been given to rise above the situation. I was going to play baseball, and with that, I would ultimately gain acceptance from the very ones who at first wanted to push me aside.

So I was all too happy when I learned Momma was capable of having us together again. I was almost fourteen when this readjustment took place and it couldn't have been a more timely change. Right away I began to feel as if I had someone on my side, someone who supported me and wanted me near. During the years we lived apart, Momma continually assured us children that she would continue working hard so one day we could all live together. Being a woman of strong will, with love for her children, she kept her word. She was now back in my life, closer than ever before, at a time when I would truly need her.

To play semipro baseball, I needed to have my summer weekends open. That was fine with Momma. She saw how important baseball was to me and did what she could to help. Momma continued to work hard and there was no easy life for us even after she got us children back. But she agreed to help arrange my work to permit free time for ball games and practices. Momma would help by doing little things to make sure I was ready to meet my ride to the game on those Saturday and Sunday afternoons. She always left a little something light for me to eat prior to each game and my uniform was part of her regular, weekly laundry; meaning, it wasn't too smelly, too often!

As the seasons passed, I began to see the progress I was making as a pitcher. In spite of getting no formal instruction, I noticed my control becoming a bit sharper even though inevitable streaks of wildness continued to pop up. My velocity increased as I matured and I continued to see the reluctance batters had as they came to the plate, fearing for their safety as well as being overmatched. I turned in one of my most impressive pitching performances against Kilmarnock, one of our league rivals. With the help of my old standby catcher Bill Clark behind the plate, I struck out 26 batters that afternoon. My effort in that game virtually gave my Lively teammates the day off. By fanning 26 batters in that nine inning game, only one Kilmarnock hitter made an out by hitting the ball into play. It was a great win for our ball club and a great moment for me, personally.

As I recall, the most highly contested rivalry within the Chesapeake League was between Lively and the team from nearby Ottoman. Today, some folks would compare this pairing to a Red Sox vs. Yankee match up, on a much smaller scale, of course. For the followers of local baseball, there was no love lost between the rooters for Lively and their opposition from six miles to the south. And what could happen that would cause this contention to heat up even more? Imagine what the repercussions would be if a primary player of one team jumped to the other side. That's exactly what happened and that player was me!

This summertime feud between Lively and Ottoman had been a lopsided affair going back several years. Ever since I started in the league, it had only been on rare occasions that Ottoman won a game against us. They were capable of fielding a talented squad, year after year; yet they seemed to have very little success when they opposed us, their fiercest rival. I remember always wanting to give my best efforts when we faced Ottoman, and this was the case with all of the players on both sides. Everyone tried to reach back for a little extra in those games when there was so much neighborhood pride at stake.

With frustration mounting, the Ottoman team had reached its limit and decided to take a course of action that had never been tried in the Chesapeake League. A few of the boys on the Ottoman ball club, along with their manager, Gilliam Lewis, contacted me prior to the start of the season, offering me cash payments on a per game basis to jump teams for what would turn out to be my final year in the league. This type of deal was practically unheard of at the time and Ottoman's proposal of fifteen dollars per game sounded like tons of money to me! Needless to say, I jumped at the chance. For me, a teenager with empty pockets, the idea of making a few bucks for playing ball was too much to resist.

I eventually played a major part in helping Ottoman gain the upper hand in the ongoing rivalry with my former team. However, my decision to accept the proposal had some far reaching effects that I didn't expect. Sure, the Ottoman folks were happy when they heard the news that I was about to join their club, but the reaction of my old teammates and the fans of Lively was one of outrage. "How could he do such a thing!" they demanded to know. Well, to me baseball was still a game and to have a chance to earn a few dollars doing what I loved to do was nothing short of unbelievable. A lot of criticism came from angry locals who saw the situation only from a baseball standpoint. To them it was a matter of loyalty There were some who felt I was too young to appreciate what the Lively team had done for me over the years and I didn't understand what team loyalty was all about. These were people who wouldn't see the full picture.

Since quitting high school, I had been working many long days cutting down trees for a local excelsior mill, earning almost nothing for my labor. I was learning some very valuable lessons about life the hard way. No one ever had to teach me about the importance of being loyal or being appreciative. Those things were inside me from the beginning.

My decision to switch teams had nothing to do with greed. It was all about need!

Playing for Lively, I was the youngest player in the Chesapeake League. My first glove and spikes were given to me by Mr. Billy Walker, Sr.

CHAPTER 4

The Tryout

Hard work, long hours and very little pay was about all I could come up with when I started adding up the company benefits of working for Bobby Chilton's excelsior mill. Cutting down trees in marshy woods provided me with just a few dollars each week and a lot of aching muscles. But I was young, and I could take it like a plow mule! That was my life after quitting high school and stepping out into the world.

Excelsior. Now, that's a word you won't hear these days. Excelsior is the fine, curly wood shavings made from stripped tree bark. In general, it was used as box packing to protect fragile items during shipping. But, with the current use of so many synthetics like Styrofoam and plastics, excelsior has gone the way of rotary telephones and record players. However, there was a bright side to all of this. Now that I wasn't going to school, I no longer had to deal with the isolation of being a social outcast each week, Monday through Friday, and I was still free to play baseball on weekends during the spring and summer. It was about this time that I began to realize that I would never be able to please everyone all of the time. As playing baseball continued to be the passion of my life, it seemed that whenever opportunity knocked on my door, my decision to move forward would be upsetting to someone.

I had just finished a good season pitching for Ottoman of the Chesapeake League. The folks of the Ottoman community were especially pleased with the beatings we gave my former team from Lively. While I still heard a few rumblings of disapproval and resentment about jumping teams a year ago, things were beginning to quiet down when opportunity came a' knocking again.

The individual who did the knocking this time was my long time advocate and supporter, Mr. Billy Walker, Sr. This was the same man who had given me my glove and my first pair of spikes just a few seasons before. Now, he was coming to me with a proposal that could help take my baseball career a step further. Mr. Walker lived in nearby Warsaw, Virginia, and was influential with the ball club there. Warsaw was a slow-paced country town located on the northern banks of the Rappahannock River, yet it was significantly larger than the tiny towns close to my home. The baseball team there was part of the Tidewater League, an advanced league of semi-professionals that had a stronger level of talent than I was accustomed. Mr. Walker felt that I was ready to take a step upward. He was convinced that the experience would be good for me and that I would be an asset to the Warsaw team. He explained how he would recommend me to the team's manager and clear the way for me to join the club in time for the start of the 1951 season.

"The talent in this league is a little better than what you're used to," he warned. "But, this will be a good chance for you to develop and prove yourself. And you can do it!" he assured.

From all I had heard, he was correct in what he told me about the Tidewater League. The league had a reputation of strong competition. The players were all young and fast, their bats were quick and only the top notch local players could make it there. I was anxious for a break, a chance to show what I could do. I had confidence in my own ability and Mr. Walker sure had faith in me, too. "Go for it!" I told myself. "What do I have to lose?"

The naysayers and doubting Thomases came out of the woodwork. This time it was the players of the Ottoman team, the Lively team and the entire Chesapeake League. It was the high school kids and lots of folks from all around the community. They all voiced their feelings about how I was

28

turning my back on the Ottoman team -- after all they had done for me. They were recalling how I deserted Lively the year before and how I showed no loyalty. They were all certain that I had no business trying something like this. They were convinced that I would fail and I should stop listening to whoever was filling my head with these wild ideas. They were sure I'd be back soon. They just weren't certain if they would ever allow me to come back, if I decided to move on.

The Tidewater League was definitely a step up. The teams all had substantial backing from sponsors who could afford the incentives the clubs needed to lure the players they wanted. All of the players had been scouted or had come highly recommended and a few of them even had some professional experience. Just about all of them were being compensated in some way. Once the Warsaw team decided to take me onboard, they presented to me what I thought was a pretty good offer. As I recall, the Tidewater Telephone Company had a significant sponsorship interest in the Warsaw team, which is why the team's offer to me was a seasonal job working for them. Of course, I knew absolutely nothing about telephones, but I could drive a truck. They agreed to pay me $150 per month just to drive a small truck around the area, chauffeuring a service technician from job to job. Compared to my other job, this was a piece of cake! It was quite convenient, too. I moved to Warsaw that spring to stay with my cousin and her husband, who had a place in town. It was a great arrangement for me. The job was easy and the pay wasn't bad. What's more, I was finding my share of success on the pitcher's mound, to boot. We faced some very talented teams from places like Richmond, Fredericksburg, Bowling Green and of course, Tappahannock, our closest and toughest rival.

Our games with them were very fierce at times. Their showcase player was an ex-major league outfielder who lived in the Tappahannock area, Clarence "Soup" Campbell. "Soup" was still a fine ballplayer and a particularly good hitter even though he was a few years beyond his career with the Cleveland Indians. I had the opportunity to face him in some crucial game situations during the season. I also had the satisfaction of striking him out a few times when the final outcome was being decided.

My season with Warsaw was just getting into high gear when my old friend, Billy Walker, Jr., came to me with an unexpected proposal. Billy, Jr., was home from college, spending the summer with his parents there in Warsaw and playing first base on the baseball team. He was a great guy to have as a teammate in addition to being a pretty fair player. He was always kidding me or teasing me about one thing or another, but with him it was always done in a good-natured way. He played on the varsity team at college and was serious about baseball. I always thought he had ideas of turning pro if he could get the right break. He and his father, Billy, Sr., seemed to always be "in the know" when it came to baseball and kept up with all the current baseball news and events. They were always among the first to hear about things, such as when and where a baseball tryout camp would be scheduled.

"Hey, Jim, are you ready to take a trip to Norfolk?" Billy, Jr., caught me off guard. "The Yankees farm team, the Norfolk Tars, is having an open tryout next week at their ballpark, Myers Field."

At first it sounded like a great idea to me. *This could be the chance I've been looking for*, I thought. But I had never been to Norfolk. I had never been anywhere, more than a few miles from home. It was easy to see that this was not a big deal for Billy, Jr., like it was for me. He brought the question up in a casual way, like it was nothing new for him.

"Sure, Billy," I answered, trying not to sound unsure. Suddenly, a storm of questions ran through my head. How will we get to Norfolk? How will we find the place? How much will it cost? Where will we stay? Now, Billy had done a little bit of traveling. He had been away from home to attend college and was much more a "man of the world" than I was. Yet, he was sensitive enough to reassure me when he noticed my hesitation.

"Yeah, Jim, I've talked to my dad about this and he's going to loan me his car and he's going to spring for the hotel room. Both of us are insisting that you come along with me. All you need to do is pack your bag along with your glove and spikes and be ready when I come by to pick you up next Friday."

Wanting to be prepared and well rested for the tryout, we drove into Norfolk late on Friday afternoon. Our plan was to check into our room before dinner, get a good night's sleep and be ready to go early on Saturday. Things went pretty much as planned except for the horrible traffic we encountered downtown. We had not anticipated the gridlock that waited for us when we arrived in the city, just when the shipyard workers, the naval base employees and the sailors were all getting off from work for the weekend. I found it hard to believe there were that many automobiles in the entire world!

Soon after dinner, Billy was ready to turn in for the night. Not me. Along with the excitement of being away from home, I felt like there were things to see and talk about before going to sleep, things that I had never seen or experienced. The thought of being over a hundred miles away from home, combined with the tall buildings, the honking automobile horns and the lights of downtown were more than enough to keep me from being sleepy. While Billy was settling into bed, I grabbed a chair and scooted it across the room, next to the window to give myself a good vantage point for checking out the city below. There were so many new and different sights for me to take in as night fell on the busy streets outside.

"Come on, man, we've got a big day ahead of us, let's get some rest," Billy urged. "I promise you, Jim, those lights and neon signs will stay on and continue to flash even after you go to bed!" Billy was getting a big laugh over my reluctance to leave the window and call it a day. "You can't take a country boy anywhere!" he declared. "Just wait until we get back home and I tell everyone how you wouldn't come to bed because you were afraid that the lights of the big city would go out if you didn't stay up to watch them!" He sat up in bed, pointed his finger at me and continued to laugh.

Billy Walker, Jr., made good on his threat to spread that story. Within a few days after returning home, it appeared that everyone in the town of Warsaw knew about my fascination with the city lights of Norfolk. They had all heard the full story, the exaggerated tale of how I could have sat at the window and watched them all night.

Early the next morning the ballfield was crowded. Young boys had come from almost everywhere and each one was full of hope, the hope of showing the scouts and coaches something special. Each one was chasing his dream, like me, wanting to become the next star for the New York Yankees. It was unlike any situation I had known. I recognized no one. Everyone was a stranger to me, except for Billy, Jr. When everyone was gathered in a large group to hear the opening instructions for the day, I took a slow look around and thought about the possibilities. Maybe I could be standing with the next Bill Dickey or a future Red Ruffing!

They split us up into groups by position. Billy went with the infielders and worked out around first base, while I went with the pitchers. I was feeling great; my arm was ready to go after just a few warm-up tosses. Suddenly, they were ready to see what I had to offer. My fastball was at its best that morning. The catcher's mitt was really popping, as a couple of older guys from the ball club stood by and watched with their arms folded. I had thrown only about 12 pitches and was just starting to find my speed and rhythm when I heard, "Okay, son, that's enough!" I stepped back a few steps to make room for the next boy to take the mound. *What could they tell about me after those few pitches? I wondered. Surely they can't know the type of pitcher I am after just two or three minutes!*

"Not bad, Coates," observed one of the men with a clipboard, who had been watching and jotting down notes. "Not bad. But we're looking for boys who can throw a little harder. We're looking for a little more speed. But thanks for coming out, we appreciate it."

What in the world could they be looking for? The puzzling question was running through my mind. A lump started to form in my throat as the disappointing words of the scout started to sink in. I stood by for a few moments and watched as another hopeful candidate delivered a few pitches. I didn't see any pitchers out there who came close to matching my fastball. And there were some who looked as if they were wasting their time, as well as the time of all the others on the field.

"What's the difference?" I asked myself out loud. My opinion didn't count. I was going back home just the same.

Of course, I was very disappointed. I felt like I had just failed my biggest test. I not only thought about how I let myself down, but how I must be a disappointment to Mr. Walker and Billy, Jr., too. I needed to remind myself that going back home to Warsaw wasn't so bad. It was still May, and I had the rest of the season in the Tidewater League ahead of me. I still had that easy job for a while longer. After that... *I guess I'll go back to work for Bobby Chilton's excelsior mill. But for now, I'll just enjoy what I have. I won't even think about cutting down trees until after the baseball season is over.*

After all of these years,
Billy Walker, Jr., and I are still close friends.

CHAPTER 5

H. P. "Percy" Dawson

There were only two days left until Christmas. The chill of another winter was beginning to make its way into the Tidewater region of Virginia. It was a cold, gray day and I wasn't feeling much like getting into the Christmas Spirit. My season of playing for Warsaw had been a good one, but on a day like this, it seemed like ancient history. Living in Warsaw, the tryout in Norfolk and working for the telephone company, all things that I experienced in recent months, now felt like recollections from years ago. I was busy cutting down trees and they were not Christmas trees. I was back to where I had left off, working for Chilton's Excelsior Company. The wind had a cold bite. But, in spite of the chill, the strenuous work had me sweating inside my heavy clothing. I knew from experience not to take off my outer coat, as the cold air blowing against my damp shirt would lead to catching a cold, or worse. The brush in these woods was thick with briars and vines. And here, like so many of the locations we selected to work, was a place only a snake or an occasional rabbit could hope to find. With the salty creeks and coves nearby, the ground was nothing but slimy mud. So the working conditions weren't exactly ideal. This day was just like any other cold day in the woods for us. The early afternoon sun had no chance of poking through the heavy clouds. There were four of us on the work crew that day and we were all busy sawing trees or trimming away branches when we heard a stranger's voice off in a distance.

"Hello! Is anyone out here?" We heard the voice of a man, but couldn't see anyone. Whoever it was, his voice sounded agitated and somewhat frantic. He yelled again. We could detect a rustling in the bushes and he seemed to be getting closer.

"Over here, buddy!" one of the boys called out to him. The stranger seemed to be struggling through the thicket, clawing his way through the brush and vines. This person surely wasn't at ease making his way through the woods. Yet, finally he emerged.

At first sight I could tell this man was exhausted. He was almost out of breath and his nerves were a bit frazzled. He trudged a few more steps into a small clearing and it was then I could see this man was dressed up. He was wearing a dark suit, a white dress shirt and a necktie!

"What in the world could he want?" I asked. "Is this man crazy?"

"Hi, boys, you sure made it hard to find you." He was trying to force a friendly smile as he began to sweep leaves and pine needles from his coat sleeves with the back of each hand. "Yes sir, you boys are a long way back off the road. No one would ever find you back here," he continued. By then we had all stopped our work and were curiously waiting to learn more. We were quietly surveying our unexpected visitor from head to toe. The briars and thorn bushes had snagged the threads in his socks and pulled a few holes in his trousers. His expensive looking leather dress shoes were coated with marsh mud, clear up to the laces. His clothes would have looked no worse if he had just finished slopping the hogs!

He was a heavy set, elderly man who could possibly pass for some sort of lawman or maybe an officer from the department of the revenue. "I'm looking for James Coates," he announced. "Would any of you boys happen to be James or know where I could find him?"

As soon as the stranger spoke I started to feel panicky. *What would he possibly want with me? Am I in some kind of trouble? Am I about to spend Christmas in jail? Perhaps, I should make a run for it.* These were the options I contemplated in a period of about two seconds.

"Yes sir, that's Jim over there," said one of the men in my crew, pointing in my direction.

"Yes, that's me," I blurted out. My throat suddenly became dry and I found it hard to swallow. "What do you need?" I asked with a gulp in my voice. The man stepped towards me, extending his arm, wanting to shake hands. I started to feel a little bit of relief. He didn't sound like someone who was about to arrest me.

"Hello, James, my name is Percy Dawson and I've come out here to find out if you'd like to play some baseball."

I stood there, stunned for a moment, still not clear on what was going on. "Sure," I finally replied. "But, I won't get off from work for another couple of hours."

The old man's brow furrowed as he showed a puzzled look. It was as if we were speaking different languages. "No, James, you don't understand. I'm not asking you to play baseball today. See, I'm a scout with the New York Yankees and I want to find out if you would be interested in signing a contract with us."

The guys on the work crew continued to stand around idly, not hiding their intentions to eavesdrop. I'm sure they were just as startled and confused as I was. It may be hard to believe, but part of my lack of comprehension stemmed from not being certain of what some of Mr. Dawson's words meant. Words like "scout" and "contract" had me confused about what he actually had in mind.

"That's right, James. We got a good look at you a while back, when you came down to Norfolk for our tryout. We think you might be what we're looking for and that's what I came out here to talk to you about," Dawson said matter-of-factly. "That's right, son. I came here today to offer you a contract to play baseball for the New York Yankees! You have heard of the Yankees, haven't you, James?" he tested me with a sarcastic tone.

"Yes sir, sure I have," I replied quickly, trying to move on from his condescending question. "Of course I have, but you need to clear up something for me. This is not making a whole lot of sense to me." I was going to let him know right away, that not all country boys would fall for a lot of fast talking.

"What do you mean, James?" It was Dawson's turn to be confused.

"Well, Mr. Dawson, it's like this. When I was in Norfolk for the tryout, no one there would give me the time of day. I threw a few pitches and before I could even get warmed up, I was told to go home. I was told I didn't throw hard enough to suit you. Now, you come all the way out here to tell me I might be just what you're looking for. I really don't know what to believe."

Mr. Dawson stood patiently, listening before he offered his explanation. "Okay, James, you have to understand. We had a lot of boys to look at, a lot of reports to review and a lot of decisions to make. I know, to you, it must seem like it took forever for us to get back with you, but things like this take time. But I'm here today to offer you five hundred dollars if you will sign this contract to play minor league baseball for the Yankees."

Not knowing what to do or say next, I just stood there staring at Mr. Dawson and the envelope he had pulled from the inside breast pocket of his coat. He held a large brown envelope by its corner and repeatedly slapped it on the open palm of his left hand. My silence continued. I felt like he was waiting for me to jump up and click my heels together with excitement. Maybe I should have. But, with all of my uncertainty, I was still dumbfounded by his proposal. *Is this man kidding me?* I wondered.

"What I want you to do, James is go with us to the Yankees' spring training camp in Sumter, South Carolina, in March and give us another chance to look at you. This will be the Yankees' minor league camp and you'll be working out with a lot of other new players, all young boys about your age. If you'll agree to do that for us, I'll write you a check for $500 today. If you can show us what we want to see and make the team coming out of camp, then we will pay you another $1000 after 90 days! It's all here for you, James. It's up to you."

Unless this fellow, Percy Dawson is playing some kind of cruel joke on me, then this is the chance of a lifetime. "Wow!" I exclaimed. *Maybe this is real after all. Maybe this is not a dream.* Five hundred dollars was more than I could imagine. And another thousand later! I had never known anyone who had that much money! I picked up on the urgency of the situation and figured I'd better say something to the old man before his offer slipped away. "Sure, Mr. Dawson, it all sounds really good to me. So, all I need to do is sign your papers and it will be all settled?"

"That's right, all settled," Mr. Dawson confirmed. "We'll give you all the details and send you a train ticket. You meet us in Sumter this spring, ready to play ball and that's all there is to it!"

"Okay, Mr. Dawson, it sounds good to me. Just show me where to sign." The boys, who had stopped working, were still following the discussion and were all in total disbelief. "Do you have a pen with you?" I asked.

"Sure I do, son" he replied while reaching again inside his coat. "But, wait a minute here, James. How old are you?" he asked, being mindful of all the regulations and technicalities.

"Seventeen," I said. "I turned seventeen back on the fourth of August, to be exact."

Mr. Dawson shook his head while he seemed to be contemplating a new course of action. *Had I said the wrong thing? Should I have lied about my age?*.

"Well, that's okay. We will just have to do things a little differently. Since you're not eighteen yet, we will have to get your parents to endorse the agreement, too. But I'm sure that won't be a problem. We just need to take these papers over to your home and show them to your mother and father and let them know what we have been discussing. I'm sure they will go along with our plan."

Dawson was telling me all of this with confidence, as if this were just a minor problem, one he had dealt with many times before. My brief time of concern was passing. "Well, we can go talk to my mother; she is still at work at the store, out here on the road. But, I don't have a father. He left us a long time ago and I can't tell you where we could find him right now."

"That will be fine," said Dawson. "I know you're pretty busy working out here, but if your co-workers can do without you for a few minutes, we will go back out to my automobile and take a ride to the store, so we can explain to your mother all about your new job offer."

No work had been done by any of the boys for the past several minutes. Everything had come to a screeching halt as soon as Percy Dawson emerged from the bushes with his proposal. "Go ahead and go, Jim," one of them ordered. "We'll be okay here. You go on now and take care of your business with this fellow. Just be sure to get back here as soon as you can and tell us how you made out." Those three young men had been hanging around quietly all the while, and now it was easy to see that their curiosity was running high.

"All right, Mr. Dawson," I suggested. "Let's go talk to Momma. I'll be back as soon as I can, boys. Like the man said, it should only take a few minutes."

Just as I had expected, Momma was receptive to the plan and as always, was very supportive, even if she was a bit unsure. Getting her signature on the contract was no problem. I think she knew somehow, that she might be helping me unlock the door to my future. She knew that baseball was the only thing that truly mattered in my life and like me, she saw this as a once-in-a-lifetime opportunity. Of course, she too was shocked by the amount of money being offered. The staggering figures of five hundred dollars now and the possibility of another thousand later had much the same effect on her as it had on me, just moments before. Momma always wanted me to have a better life. She always wanted what was best for me. She hoped this would be her chance to help me have that life.

Momma and I both signed the multiple copies of the contract and passed them back to Percy, trusting him and hoping all along that he was on the level with us. We were both praying that there was nothing hidden in the fine print that would be cause for regret in the future. Momma and I knew absolutely nothing about closing a business deal. Yet, we moved forward that day, on nothing more than a hope, a prayer and trust in a man we had just met minutes before, a man named Percy Dawson.

"James Alton Coates," he read from the bottom of the page as he made a final inspection of the agreement document.

"Jim" is what we all call him around here," Momma interjected. "Everybody knows him as Jim."

"Okay, Jim," Percy concurred. "That's it for right now. We will have someone get in touch with you folks to keep you posted on the details. Here is your check for five hundred dollars, and I wish you both a happy, wonderful Christmas. And, Jim, there is one more thing, be extra careful working out there with those fellows. Remember, starting today, you belong to the New York Yankees!"

CHAPTER 6

You Have to Start Somewhere!

"It's all about how you spend your time," a wise man once said. "For a boy at the circus, it will fly by. For a man in prison, it will seem like forever." Now, don't get the wrong idea. I never had to go to prison, but there were times during the winter of 1951-52 when it felt like time had slowed down to a crawl. The cold months of January and February were slow to pass and March seemed like it was never going to come. Since I signed the contract with Mr. Dawson and the Yankees back in December, time had been moving along at the speed of cold molasses.

On the other hand, the news about my signing with the Yankees had spread quickly. Everyone in the community had an opinion and a prediction about my chances of staying in professional baseball. I began to wonder if I lived in the land of negative thinking. It was difficult for me to say for sure if the folks in my hometown actually wanted to see me fail or if they truly felt that I had no business leaving home to seek my fortune in pro baseball. Regardless of the basis of their thinking, almost everyone in the county seemed to be sure that I would be home soon. Most of them were certain that I would be back working my old job and trying to catch on with one of the local semi pro teams.

But the big day finally arrived. It was now time to leave home. The days of speculation and suspense were over. In spite of the excitement and apprehension that had been churning inside of me for the past three months, my day of departure was like I expected, nothing spectacular.

There was no noise in the neighborhood about my leaving, no big send off. There were only a couple of supportive hugs from Momma and a few nagging remarks from my brother, Slim, who continually pestered me about running late. He was absolutely convinced that we were going to miss the south bound, morning train out of Richmond. Momma was quiet and thoughtful as she moved about the house. I had no doubts that she was pulling for me to find success. Like I mentioned before, she always wanted the best for me. However, she was also aware that I was the first in our family to leave home and be faced with such a rare opportunity. She knew about the pressure on me to do well and didn't want me to return home to the locals who were waiting to see me fail.

After a near sleepless night, we rose early on the long awaited morning. I felt certain I would overlook something important as I double-checked my luggage. Concentration didn't come easily that morning as Slim seemed to be determined to test my patience. I was forced to keep my cool with him, knowing he was my only means of transportation to Richmond and that this was, hopefully, the last favor I would need to ask of him for a long time. He was being the typical bossy, older brother. He had agreed to drive me to the railroad station. Yet, he anxiously paced about the house, telling me over and over to hurry up. He advised me repeatedly as to what I should pack and what I should leave behind.

When the four of us finally drove away that cold March morning, we were quite a sight to see, I assure you. The Beverly Hillbillies had nothing on the Coates family! Slim was behind the wheel of his 1931 Chevrolet with me riding shotgun beside him on the front seat. Momma and Madeline, Slim's wife of just a few months, squeezed their way into the back, filling that old car to capacity. There was no room left for luggage in that old jalopy, so we had my suitcases lashed to the front fenders. Uncle Jed and the Clampett family could have taken a lesson or two from us on how to pack a vehicle for a long drive. We were loaded up and on our way! We made it to Richmond with time to spare.

Once I was aboard the train, I had planned to get comfortable, just sit back and relax for the next several hours. But relaxation was out of the question. The train ride to Sumter was a totally new experience. For me, it was a journey into the unknown. Had I been traveling to London or Paris, it would not have been a more daunting or unnerving undertaking. I felt a bit of relief when I managed to get off the train at the right stop. *If only the balance of my venture would go this well.*

The chilly spring winds of South Carolina were nothing new for me. The climate of the area was a lot like the March weather I had left back home, but that's where the similarities stopped. The other passengers at the railroad station all looked as if they knew where to go and what to do next. Not me. I just stood around on the platform, contemplating my next move when a man approached me and asked if I were James Coates. He grabbed one of my travel bags as he introduced himself and informed me he was there to give me a ride to the training complex. In what seemed like no time, we were there. And even then, there wasn't a familiar face to be seen.

There were young ball players there from all over the Eastern United States. They were all about my age and each one was there with hopes of surviving the cuts and making the team to start the season in April. We were all there to compete for spots on the Yankees' Class D team which would be based in Olean, New York. The club was part of the Pony League, the Pennsylvania-Ontario-New York League. The simpler, shorter version of the league's name was preferred for the convenience of everyone involved, especially by sports writers. This was the lowest of all the levels of professional baseball. Yet, I was positively impressed by what I saw shortly after arriving.

We were soon gathered on the training field, about 35 of us, for a short orientation. All of us rookies were in complete silence as we listened for our orders of operation. It was difficult to pick up each detail as we were being told about the rules and routines of camp. It sounded like a lot of information for a bunch of nervous young boys to digest, but I'm sure I wasn't the only one struggling to hear it all. As we stood shoulder to shoulder in that group of hopeful athletes, I wondered if this was the first trip away from home for any of the others. *Could there be anyone from Virginia besides me? Did anyone travel as far as I did?* My mind was filled with questions while I was trying to listen attentively to the coach.

"Okay, fellows, be sure to be done with breakfast early and be on the team bus by nine o'clock. The bus will leave the hotel at nine o'clock, sharp! It's your job to be on time. After our workout and team meeting, the bus will take us back to the hotel. You will eat your meals at the hotel. Be sure to sign your meal ticket and include your room number, so the ball club can pick up your tab."

All of those instructions sound simple to me today. But, for me, a backwoods country boy at seventeen, it was a lot to keep straight.

This was a city-owned complex used for local scholastic athletics. The schools had a working agreement with the Yankee organization for temporary use in the spring. There were two well kept baseball fields on the site along with locker rooms and showers which were far better and more up to date than anything I had seen while playing baseball back home. I was quite impressed by the place. I had no idea that my positive impressions and my good feelings about being in camp were going to disappear so soon.

Our first scheduled workout was the scene of one of the most humiliating situations of my entire life. The first order of the day was the distribution of our team uniforms. We were all issued our cap, belt, uniform top, pants and stirrup socks.

"What in the world are stirrup socks?" I asked myself. The other guys seemed to be okay with the terminology, but I had never heard of them. I got suited up and had everything on except my shoes and socks.

Now, what am I supposed to do with these? I thought, as I held them up, one in each hand. I stared at the extra long, dark colored hose. It looked like someone had cut away the front foot area as well as the heel on each of them! Only a small strap remained, which would run under the bottom of my foot.

"There's got to be more to it than this!" I assured myself. "But, what now?" My hesitation must have been very noticeable. My ignorance was showing.

"Just put them on over your other socks and pull your pants legs down over them. That's all there is to it," an unidentified voice offered.

It sure sounded easy enough, so I decided to give it a try. *I'll put on my other socks first, and then the stirrups,* I figured. The only other socks I had was the pair I had worn with my street clothes. They were bright, colorful, argyle socks with a large bold diamond pattern, very much the typical style of the time, but certainly not the style for baseball.

"Get a load of those feet!"

"Take a look at those wild socks!"

"Check this guy out!"

The reactions of disbelief came from all over the locker room. I had unintentionally given every member of the team the laugh of his life. Guys were coming from everywhere to see it for themselves. If embarrassment could be fatal, I would have died on the spot. If only I could have jumped into the nearest locker or under the closest bench, I would still be there today!

The frolic was interrupted. "No, buddy, you need to put those over your white sanitary socks," a helpful voice chimed in. "Here, I have a few extra pairs of sanitaries. You can use a pair of mine today."

Still today, I remember that kind gesture extended to me by that boy, a teammate from Connecticut who had extra socks to offer. However, his help came just a little too late for me to save face. The damage had already been done. I was already the laughing stock of the camp.

Starting with that incident I began to feel farther away from home than ever. I really felt out of place. I had suddenly been labeled a bumbling country hick, the boy who didn't know how to put his socks on. I was embarrassed and depressed by it all. Maybe I let it bother me more than it should. *Maybe the folks back home were right after all*, I began to wonder. *I'm not cut out for this. I don't need to be around people like these guys. Maybe I don't have any business being here.* Doubt was filling my mind. I felt like packing up and heading for home! The situation really had me in the dumps. I thought about overcoming it all by turning in an impressive performance on the field each day. But, how could I be at my best when I was the target of so many jokes and critical remarks?

I needed someone to turn to, someone to talk some sense into me. I was in this by myself so that someone would have to be me. It was time for me to take a step back and rethink things.

I couldn't go back home. That would give a lot of people the pleasure of being right about me. I surely didn't want to face them. Not to mention, I didn't have enough money to make the trip. As far as playing baseball goes, it was clear that I was just as much of a baseball player as any of those loud-mouthed boys in the camp. I'll just have to go on letting people say what they want. I've been doing that for a long time already.

Stick with it, Jim. You have to start somewhere, I thought, attempting a little self discipline. *Don't let a stupid locker room incident get in the way of doing what you want to do.*

The next morning I was up early. The conversation I had with myself was helping. I was pushing myself to be ready, to give it my best for at least one more day. My personal pep talk had made me determined to give this training camp another shot and to play my best.

"There are lots of boys from all around the country who would give anything to be in my place," I said. "After all, I'm a Yankee!"

After I dressed out and headed for the field, I took another look at my uniform and took notice of each item I was wearing. Most of those items were new to me and represented my new team, the Yankees. But there, still with me, were my old spikes and my Indian head glove, things given to me by Mr. Billy Walker, Sr., years ago. The glove was tattered and worn. The shoes were showing a lot of heavy wear. They were very familiar to me. These items had been with me through winning and losing, through thick and thin. I was quickly reminded of some people back home in Virginia who had supported me throughout the years. I was sure they still believed in me.

CHAPTER 7

This Is Professional Baseball?

I'm not really sure how I did it, but somehow I made it through that first spring training in South Carolina. It was a struggle for me the entire time. I could hardly wait for camp to end so we could head north and start the season. Playing out the schedule with a game every day had to be better than the rigors of training camp.

My head was cluttered with a truckload of worries. Naturally, I was unsettled, being young and away from home for an extended time. But, along with that, I had money on my mind. I had been promised a check for $1000 if I could hang on with the team through spring training and I was striving to do everything I needed to do to make sure I got it.

When the camp opened, there were about 35 of us there. After just a few weeks, cuts were being made and some of the boys were released by the club and sent home. Each of those boys had been called aside by the manager and given the dreaded bad news. So, for the fortunate ones, those of us who survived, it was a matter of "no news was good news." As long as we didn't hear anything, we were fine. The roster of players in camp had been whittled down to about two dozen, and I began to have a hint of certainty that I would be starting the season with the team.

I was never conceited or brash enough to think I had a place on the team right from the start, but I could easily see that none of the other pitchers in camp were throwing the baseball nearly as well as I was. None of them had a pitch that could keep up with my fastball. They couldn't match my velocity or my control. At the same time, I needed to keep in mind that who made the team wasn't up to me. The fate of each of us was in the hands of someone else, so this was no time for me to be counting unhatched eggs. But, with just a few weeks before the start of the season, I was finally handed the long-awaited check which gave me a whole new outlook on life. The Yankees had finally come through and I could hardly believe my eyes! There in my hands was a check for one thousand dollars made out to me, James A. Coates! The numbers on that piece of paper were staggering to me. I felt like a millionaire or at least king for a day. But, aside from the excitement of cashing this big check, I saw a commitment being made by the Yankees. I saw the New York Yankees making an investment in me, a thousand dollar investment that suggested I might be in their plans for the future. How far in their future, I couldn't say for sure, but I knew full well that I would soon be making the trip to Olean, New York.

Another good feeling I had at the time came from the relief of not having to face any of the guys back home who had predicted an early return for me. I was denying them any satisfaction for a while longer, at least. This was somewhat spiteful of me, but the doubts I heard before I left home continued to be a driving force behind me which caused me to keep pushing hard to succeed. I hoped never to return home to hear any of them say they were right about judging my talents or predicting my future. Now I started to look forward to my return to Virginia, having a full season of professional baseball under my belt. That was a lot more than many of them ever envisioned for me and certainly a lot more than any of them had ever achieved for themselves.

The 1952 Pony League season was just a couple of days from starting when our team bus pulled out of Sumter, South Carolina. It was hardly daylight that spring morning when that old bus hit the highway, loaded to capacity. It was filled not just with players and their luggage and equipment but with a full load of hopes and dreams. All of us onboard were hopeful and excited about the season ahead. We were anxious to prove our own skills as well as to check out the talent around the rest of the league. We were facing a bus ride of about 18 hours if we stayed on schedule and had no troubles or delays. Well, so much for wishful thinking. After just a few hours on the road, we ran into a little unanticipated problem.

We had crossed over into North Carolina and were nearing the Virginia border when the motor in our old bus started to make a knocking, clanking sound. It was the swan song for that old bucket of bolts. After just a few seconds, that awful noise and the bus both came to a stop. There we were, stranded on the side of the highway in the middle of Nowhere, North Carolina! Thank goodness for good weather. For about four hours we sat on a grassy bank on the roadside waiting for help to arrive. *How frustrating and embarrassing! So, this is professional baseball?* I asked myself. Not only were there two dozen of us ball players sitting on the ground next to an old, broken down motor coach, but everyone driving by knew who we were. Our name, "Olean Yankees," was boldly painted on the side of the bus in big colorful letters for everyone to see. This was just another part of being a Yankee I had not expected. Eventually we boarded another bus which was sent to rescue us. We had no Moses to lead us and received no manna from above, yet we were once again on our way to find our own promised land.

There was still a little winter nip in the air when we arrived in upstate New York, but we were all aware that it was springtime and time to get the season started. After playing just a handful of games, I began to realize that for me personally, there was nothing threatening or intimidating about the level of play in the Pony League. To me, it seemed many of our games were similar to what I had experienced back home as a semi-pro player in the Chesapeake League. The big difference for me was the paycheck I was getting on the first and fifteenth of every month.

After just a few seconds,
that awful noise and the bus came to a stop.
I'm second from the left.

We were well into the season when it dawned on me that my pitching was much the same as what it had been in the semi-pro leagues. I was throwing the ball really well and getting a lot of strikeouts, but I was looking for more. It was disappointing to find that at this level of baseball there was hardly any time put towards teaching and instruction. Normally, the team had only the field manager running the show and he had to do it all. In addition to being the manager, he was our batting coach, our pitching coach, and also handled our transportation and lodging. He even had to be a disciplinarian for some of the boys. His job required him to wear a lot of different hats. So it was easy to see why one on one instruction was practically out of the question. It was also easy to see that he was not a pitcher by trade and had very little help to offer in that area. As pitchers we were all on our own and helped each other as much as we could. I was still waiting for someone to come along who would spend time with me to work on proper pitching mechanics and techniques. I wanted to learn to use the right pitches in certain game situations. I wanted to learn how to think like a pitcher. After all, this was professional baseball, right?

I saw a lot of action that season and I felt like I took advantage of my opportunities, such as they were. I pitched well and noticed improvement in my control. I was told my fastball was probably the best in the league. I worked 226 innings that year and averaged a strikeout per inning. With this, I drew a lot of attention from around the league and from within the Yankee organization. They all seemed to be pleased with my fastball and my number of strikeouts, which was about twice as many as my bases on balls.

As the schedule was winding down, my confidence was given a big boost when some of the coaches and scouts spoke to me about returning to training camp next spring and what I should expect in the higher levels of the Yankee system. It all sounded great to me. It was music to my ears! Now, all I needed to do was make it through the off season back home. *That won't be too difficult*, I told myself. *There will be a few people there who will see that they were wrong about me!*

Like so many of the men of coastal Virginia, my brother, Slim, made his living from the water. He was a commercial waterman who worked the Rappahannock River and the Chesapeake Bay to catch some of the world's finest fish. Each year during the fall and winter I was in need of seasonal work to hold me over financially while I wasn't playing ball. Slim arranged a deal with the captain of his fishing boat for me to take a spot on the boat's crew at the end of baseball season. This deal turned out to be steady work for me for several years while I was playing in the minor leagues. It was hard work for sure. Getting up before dawn, fighting the cold winds on the river and pulling nets loaded with fish into the boat while ice was forming on the washboards was no picnic, even for the toughest of men. But the work paid my bills and kept me in good physical shape, as you can imagine. After a month or two of working those huge nets, I would be eagerly looking forward to spring training so I could give my body a break from the hard labor of being a fisherman.

My second spring training took me farther away from home. That year, 1953, I trained in Ocala, Florida, at the Yankees' regular minor league camp. This camp was for players in all classes of the Yankee farm system except for the first year boys. The whole concept of spring training was nowhere near as unnerving for me as it had been a year earlier. I was a lot better prepared mentally and emotionally for my second camp. It wasn't like I was a seasoned veteran by no means, yet I did have some idea about what to expect, as well as what was expected of me. About two-thirds of the guys from the Olean team of last year would be returning, so that gave me some assurance that I would be seeing some familiar faces when we reported for training again in March.

I survived the training ordeals of that spring and then found myself assigned to Joplin, Missouri, of the class C, Western Association. Again, I was the workhorse of the pitching staff, working about 220 innings for the year while being effective enough to keep my earned run average below three and a half. I found the hitters in that circuit to be more advanced with quicker bats than what I had seen in the Pony League. When all was said and done for the season, I felt pretty good about my performance and I also got more positive feedback from the farm system staff, which made me confident about being back with them next year. In the meantime, I would be going back to my job on the fishing boat, but I would be returning home with another feather in my cap, one that would show everyone that I had made it another year with the Yankees.

When spring rolled around the following year, 1954, I had a surprise waiting for me at the end of training camp. Since this was the start of my third season with the Yankees and since I had experienced another good spring, I was expecting to follow the normal path of progression and get a promotion to class B level to begin the season. However, I was unexpectedly assigned to the Yankees top minor league team in Binghamton, New York. The Binghamton Triplets, as they were called, were part of the Eastern League, a class A league which was only one step below the major leagues. What a nice promotion that would be! But, it was all short-lived. It appeared at first that I would be skipping a level and jumping from class C to A. As things soon unfolded, I found myself leaving the Triplets after appearing in just two games and heading down south to the Norfolk Tars of the Piedmont League.

Leaving the Binghamton team after such a short visit was a little disappointing, yet I tried to see it as another shot of confidence from the Yankee farm staff. Norfolk certainly wasn't the worst place for me to be. I was playing in the Piedmont League, which was a well established and highly regarded class B league and it wasn't as if the major leagues were out of reach from that point. Quite a few New York Yankees who had obtained stardom at the major league level had spent some time with the Tars. Yogi Berra, Phil Rizzuto, Vic Raschi and Whitey Ford had each made a stop in Norfolk on their career path to the top.

Then too, it felt pretty good to be so close to home. It was only about a two and a half hour drive to get back up to Virginia's Northern Neck, which meant, a quick trip home on an off day wasn't difficult to arrange. Besides, I was earning a net salary of 63 dollars, which was paid twice a month, (yes, you read it correctly.....$63) and I was on my way to having another successful season as a professional, finishing with nine games won and only six losses.

I stopped long enough to ponder my situation. *My chances are looking pretty good*, I thought to myself. *Life ain't too bad!*

NORFOLK TARS, INC.
PAYROLL ACCOUNT

PAID

No. 98

NORFOLK, VA. _May 18_ 19_57_ 68-716 / 514

PAY TO THE ORDER OF _James C_ .... $ _63.21_

Sixty-three and ⁸⁰/₁₀₀ .... DOLLARS

68-716

SOUTHERN BANK OF NORFOLK
NORFOLK, VA.

NORFOLK TARS, INC.
PAYROLL ACCOUNT

Roy Grunges

PRESIDENT · SECRETARY · TREASURER
GENERAL MANAGER

Can you believe it? I got two of these every month!

While at home during the winter months, I was always ready
to help out in the kitchen whenever Momma baked a cake!

58

CHAPTER 8

When the Student Is Ready

In the spring of 1955, I found myself starting another year of Yankees baseball, minor league style. But this year was a little different from other years past. I felt different. My attitude was one of familiarity. My approach was one of confidence and hope. I felt like I had the training camp routine down fairly well and I carried with me some silent expectations that this season would be a good one. After stringing together three solid seasons with the organization, it was apparent that they must be pleased with my development so far. However, I realized that this was not the time to allow my newly found sense of comfort to get out of hand. I would need to keep my confidence in check and focus on the task at hand. Naturally, I was anxious to move up to the next level, but I made sure to remind myself that I was still learning to play the game and learning to play it the Yankee way.

At the end of spring training in April, I was quickly dispatched to Birmingham of the Southern League to start the 1955 regular season. This assignment was no promotion for me, but I was assured that it was only a temporary move. "Just a matter of numbers," I was told. "The club needs to make a few late hour roster moves and then you will be moved up," they claimed. The club was true to its word and after just four games with Birmingham, I was shipped out to Binghamton, New York, once again, where my stay the previous year had been much too short.

The Binghamton Triplets were the top level farm team of the Yankees for the eastern half of the country, so this assignment was a pleasant one to get. The team had a history of success in the Eastern League, particularly in recent times. They had won back to back league championships in 1952 and 1953 and still had sufficient talent to finish near the top of the standings since then.

The manager, a true veteran of major league baseball, was George "Snuffy" Stirnweiss. George was a former second baseman who had seen quite a few seasons as a Yankee regular. He was a guy who seemed to have a good handle on the fundamentals of play as well as experience on how to do things the Yankee way. I was certain a good season was just around the corner.

Up to this point in my career, my command of pitches had been sporadic. My control seemed to come and go. There had been times when I truly had no idea where my pitches were going. For instance, there was a game in Joplin, where manager Buddy Mick left me in the game to walk 12 batters in the first inning. He made a quick trip out to the mound and stayed only long enough to tell me, "You'll have to die to get taken outta this game!"

The following year, when I was with Norfolk my control was not nearly the issue it had been before. I still had no real accuracy to brag on, but my control was a little more "under control." For me, control seemed to rise and fall, much like the tides back home in coastal Virginia.

However, once I arrived in Binghamton in '55, things began to click. My accuracy started to fall into place again and my fastball was cracking just as fast as ever. The Triplets were having a pretty good year overall as well. We drew some fairly large crowds at old Johnson Field, a stadium which was actually located in Johnson City, New York, a town which, along with Binghamton and Endicott, formed the triple cities our team represented. The Triplets' fans there were very supportive and enthusiastic and stuck by us to the end. Many watched and shared our disappointment when we were eliminated in the first round of the league playoffs.

For me personally, it was my most rewarding professional season to date. I made progress with my control and was doing a better job of "hitting my spots" on a more consistent basis. This all resulted in a record of thirteen wins and eight losses and a respectable earned run average of 2.77. I was fortunate to end the year with 186 strikeouts, which was enough to lead all pitchers of the Eastern League in that category.

In spite of the success I found in Binghamton, I continued to sense that I was finding my way on my own. I saw myself giving a solid pitching performance game after game using nothing more than sheer intimidation and a fastball that most hitters were unable to get around on. I knew there was a lot more for me to learn and that I had a long way to go to reach my potential. If I were to be the pitcher I knew I could be, I needed someone to guide me. The master I was searching for, that special man with the rare combination of experience, insight and a willingness to teach had yet to surface. Little did I know how close this person was or how soon he would appear. I was unaware that this long awaited, destined encounter would occur in a city close to my home, the city where my journey of professional baseball first began, the city where I caught the train to my first spring training: Richmond, Virginia.

* * *

The Yankees minor league system underwent a realignment prior to the opening of the 1956 season. For years, the Denver Bears of the Pacific Coast League had been the only triple-A team in the system while the Yankees' top farmhands in the eastern half of the United States were stationed at Binghamton of the AA Eastern League. Now the Eastern League was definitely a league with a reputation of great play and a high level of talent and was often a direct source of players for the major leagues. However, it was still, technically a level below AAA. Seeing an advantage to be gained by operating a AAA team in the East, the Yankees seized the opportunity to place an entry in the International League at Richmond. The Virginians or V's, as they were called, had been in the IL for a couple of years with no major league affiliation. The club had languished at the bottom of the standings during that time in spite of the leadership of manager, Luke Appling. But once the Yankees settled in Richmond, the Virginians quickly became the showcase team of the circuit. Even with top quality players and winning seasons, the locals in the Capital City of the South must have continued to harbor hard feelings when it came to having Yankees of any kind occupying a part of their city. The poor attendance was proof. While the Virginians were consistently among the winning teams of the league, their numbers at the turnstiles we at the bottom.

During spring, I was delighted to get the word about the Yankees new AAA team in Richmond and to learn that I was headed there to start the season. This meant that I would be even closer to home than I had been two summers ago when I was with Norfolk. I also recognized that playing in the International League left room for just one more promotion. Any advancement from this level meant a call-up to the majors.

Could this be the year? I wondered.

I knew within myself that it was a possibility, but I had a job to concentrate on right there in Richmond. "First things first" was going to be my working motto.

It was to my very good fortune that the Yankees chose one of the truly great pitchers of the team's history to be the manager of this new team.. They had decided upon Eddie Lopat, a left-handed pitcher who had recently completed a twelve-year career in the major leagues, with two-thirds of those seasons spent in a Yankee uniform. His appointment to be the Virginians' skipper was somewhat unusual as well as unexpected. He had been an active player until the conclusion of the previous season, working more than 130 innings for the year to close out his career. He had split the campaign between New York and the Baltimore Orioles, making it a disappointing ending for Ed, who truly wanted to finish up as a Yankee. But being back in the Yankee chain with a new job spoke volumes about the trust, and confidence his employers had in him.

By baseball tradition, few former pitchers are ever selected to be field managers at any level. It's an unwritten policy that still applies today. It's often been said that position players, especially catchers will make the best managers. They get a better look at the entire field and the execution of each play. Thus, position players supposedly get a better education of how the game is to be played by an entire team. Well, so much for that way of thinking! Ed Lopat was definitely an exception to that rule. He came to Richmond with no coaching or managerial experience; yet, his leadership and knowledge were qualities that were quickly seen by anyone working with him.

And wow, what a teacher he was! This man had to be the one! Now, my long wait was finally over. The guy with the experience, the know-how and the all-important ability to teach had arrived. It was Lopat!

In addition to his responsibilities as field manager, Ed set aside time to work with me, one on one. We were able to communicate with each other from the very start. We hit it off from a personality standpoint as well, in that we both took a serious approach to our work. He seemed to take a special interest in me and often made time for us to just talk about pitching. We discussed things such as mechanics, pitch location, holding runners on base and pitch selection. Ed wanted me to start thinking like a pitcher. He impressed on me that it was my job to outthink the batter and not just simply overpower him each time he came to the plate. He spent long periods observing my delivery and pointed out how I threw from different angles on each pitch.

"This we'll correct by having you groove your throws and shortening your stride," he assured. "All you need now, Jim, is a good slider to add to the mix!"

So it was under his watchful eye that I began working on that pitch right away. It was a different type of breaking ball for me, one that in later years I would resort to in many tough situations.

All of this time of personal instruction was very special to me. I was amazed by his knowledge and grateful for his time and patience. All along, I knew I was learning from one of the best and I accepted it all from Ed as a special gift, from a special teacher, a man who had won 166 games in the major leagues, plus four more in World Series play. He was a man who knew how to pitch and how to win. He had the numbers to prove it. Ed Lopat did so much to help me become a pitcher. He also made me a firm believer in the old proverb that says, "When the student is ready, the teacher will appear."

My season at Richmond was an unusual one. Thanks to Lopat my confidence was high although my effectiveness was questionable. As my tutor, he gave me a lot of new ideas and some different pitching techniques to try out, but as my manager, he also gave me the freedom to make a mistake as long as he knew I was giving my best effort. If I were to give a hitter the type of pitch he was expecting or if my control was absent for the day, he would always show patience and have some encouragement to offer. He insisted that I continue to use the things we had worked on together and assured me that things would soon come together.

On occasions my wildness would show up out of no-where. As the season was winding down in August, I found myself with a losing record of six wins and twelve losses and with quite a few more walks than strikeouts. For me, it had been a great year for learning, but not so good for applying the principles I had been taught. By the numbers, it had been my worst season in professional baseball. However, it was about to become a monumental year when you judge it by the unexpected.

I was in front of my locker, peeling off a sweat-soaked Virginians' uniform top when one of the coaches yelled to me across the clubhouse.

"Coates! Hey, Coates! The Skipper wants to see you in his office right away!"

"Oh my, gosh!" I mumbled under my breath. "This can't be good. Where are they going to send me, now?"

I grabbed a fresh, dry towel and slowly made my way over to Lopat's office. It was with a lot of apprehension that I opened the door. I poked my head inside.

"Uh, yeah, Skip. I was told to come see you."

"Yeah, Jim, that's right. Come on in and have a seat," Ed offered. "I have something to talk over with you."

By the tone of his voice, I didn't feel like he was too displeased with me, so I plopped myself down on the metal, folding chair, directly in front of his desk.

"Well, Jim, they've made a call for you. For the next few days the Yankees will be stopping in Boston for a few games. It's all part of this long road trip they're on. They want you to meet them on the road at Fenway Park in Boston. Can you be ready?"

I became lightheaded, and a little dizzy as I sat in that chair, trying to make sense of what Ed had just told me.

Did I hear him correctly? I questioned myself. *Did he say what I think he said?*

For a moment I was silent. I was shocked.

"Well, yeah. Sure thing, Skipper," I managed to mutter. "I'll be ready to go. You better believe I'll be ready to go!"

Is it always darkest just before dawn?

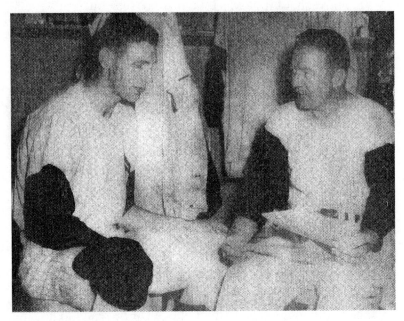

I am shown here with my mentor, Eddie Lopat. We were able to communicate with each other from the very start.

CHAPTER 9

Walking on Air

It was a long time ago: 1956. Yet, I seem to recall the man's name was Bruce Henry. I believe it was Bruce who met me at the airport in Boston, and it was his handshake that gave me one of the few welcomes I would receive that day, my first in the big leagues. Bruce was the traveling secretary for the Yankees and it was his job to meet me, greet me and drive me to the ballpark. This was my first time in a city of this size and just passing through the bustling airport was a daunting experience in itself. I had never seen so many folk rushing about in different directions, each one loaded down with an assortment of suitcases, briefcases and diaper bags. This was Logan Airport, the old, established hub of passenger transportation for the northeast. It had just under gone a name change from Boston Airport to Logan a few weeks prior to my arrival. Regardless of the name, it was a scene of chaos and confusion. I had no idea at the time that this place would be a spot I would use to land and depart many times in the years to come.

It was comforting to find that Bruce knew his way around town, because I sure didn't. He got us out of the airport parking area and zigzagged his way through the Beantown traffic and drove us to a reserved parking space at Fenway Park in almost no time. He had performed this part of his job many times before. The small talk we had along the way was congenial, even if his questions about my baseball résumé and my hometown sounded routine and artful. I soon realized that this was to be the last cordial conversation I would have for a while, as there was certainly no warm reception waiting for me in the Yankee clubhouse.

As a team, the Yankees were in the best of situations. They were in the driver's seat, having already won the American League pennant. They were looking forward to the upcoming World Series which would start in less than two weeks, so they were just "playing out the string." It didn't require a genius to figure out why they had me there. The heat was off. They had the luxury of coasting to the finish line. Because none of the remaining games were critical, there was no need to expose any of the regular, everyday players to injuries or to overwork the pitching staff. This opened up a real need for guys like me to come up to the big league club. Of course, it was a chance for me to test the waters at the top level, but even more, they needed more pitchers to simply burn up the innings. They would continue to use their regular rotation of starting pitchers -- Whitey Ford, Bob Turley, Johnny Kucks and Don Larsen -- but their pitching for each appearance would be limited to no more than about five innings. That way, each starter worked enough innings of a game to get credit for a win, with follow-up work from relief pitchers who would be called upon to come in and protect the lead.

In spite of the time I had spent in the Yankee system, I had never been around any of the players on the big club. Naturally, I was familiar with many of their names, but as a farmhand I had only seen a few of them during occasional exhibition games along the way. Consequently, my new teammates were a bunch of strangers to me. I didn't see a single familiar face among them. As I recall seeing Casey Stengle for the first time, I thought he must have been a coach of some sort or maybe even a clubhouse attendant. It never occurred to me that the waddling old fellow could be the team's famous manager. I'm not quite clear on what a major league manager should look like, but I thought Yogi Berra came a lot closer to the image I had in mind. My first impression of Yogi left me thinking that he must be running the show. He seemed to be doing a lot of the talking and he appeared to have something to say to almost everyone. Maybe it was his stubby physique or possibly his self-assured look of experience that swayed my thinking, but regardless, I would have mistaken Yogi to be the manager before ever guessing Casey was the real boss of the operation.

To gain any acceptance at all, a rookie needs to know his place, stay in it and keep his mouth shut and that's exactly what I wanted to do! Unsure of the routine leading up to game time, I dressed quietly at my locker and tried to take in as much of the noisy activity going on around me as I could. The conversations, the laughing and the assortment of characters, everything was all very dreamlike. It felt unreal to be there.

I finally got up the nerve to follow some of the others away from the locker area and out to a tunnel connecting the clubhouse to our dugout. There were a few of the guys already hanging around the bench, laughing and needling each other with all the confidence and ease of a team that had the league championship in the bag. Not sure of what to do, I waited around nervously, staring out at the field, standing out of the way. Meanwhile, my navy blue Yankee jacket warmed me and kept me from giving much thought to the chill of the autumn New England air. Finally, the pitching coach, Jim Turner, strolled over to me, introduced himself and suggested that I just take it easy, loosen up a little on the field with some stretching and make sure to be in the dugout for the start of the game.

Throughout my body I was noticing a strange tightness. A nervous excitement was beginning to take over. I decided I had better take advantage of the chance to loosen my arms and legs with a few light stretching exercises on the grass along the leftfield foul line. That's when I got a sudden, unexpected pat on the back. "Welcome to the big time, Jim!"

I spun around quickly, startled that anyone would call me by my name. It was my friend, Jerry Lumpe, an infielder who had just been called up to the Yankees, just a few days earlier. Seeing him was a pleasant surprise. Jerry, a friendly sort of fellow from Missouri, had been with me the past couple of years at Birmingham and Richmond. After the quick greeting, he trotted away to continue his pre-game work with the other fielders.

I appreciated his taking time to speak to me, however, since no one else there seemed to know my name or had bothered to ask.

The Red Sox committed a couple of errors in the top of the first, allowing us to get ahead 3-0 after one inning. My buddy Jerry had gotten another chance to start at shortstop. He had been doing very well since his call up to New York and had provided us with an early spark that night. As our leadoff hitter, he reached base on an error by Boston shortstop Billy Klause and scooted around to score our first run on a single by Mickey Mantle. Jerry wanted to take full advantage of his opportunity to play, knowing the possibility of securing a regular spot in the Yankee infield was not out of his reach. The word circulating around baseball for the past several weeks was about the likely retirement of Phil Rizzuto, the great shortstop who had held down the position since the early forties. All the more reason for Jerry to play hard.

Bob Turley, our starting pitcher, seemed to be cruising along with no problems through the first two innings. From the bench, I was attentively observing the Red Sox batters since this was my job for now, studying each of them, watching their swings and trying to detect any tendencies any of them may show on various pitches.

Mantle made it even more enjoyable with one of his long homeruns in the top of the second, increasing our lead to 4-0. Even going into the home half of the third, that margin appeared to be adequate with Turley in dominating form. But, my goodness, how quickly things can change!

"Bullet Bob" couldn't get anyone out in the bottom of the third. Ted Lepcio started the Boston barrage with a slicing line drive to leftfield. Fortunately for us, Yogi chased it down and quickly got off an accurate throw back to the infield in time to nail Lepcio at second base as he tried to stretch his hit into a double. After that first out, it was "Katie bar the door!" The Sox attacked Turley with one hit after another. Stengle finally had to go to his bullpen for right-hander, Sonny Dixon. Sonny managed to get Lepcio, who had led off the inning to tap a slow bouncing infield grounder to get that elusive final out, but by that time it was too late. The Red Sox had scored six runs on seven hits and held a 6-4 lead over us after three innings. As the fourth inning was about to start, I was instructed by Coach Turner to head out to the bullpen. I wasted no time in getting down there and without saying a word to anyone, I quickly found an open seat in the line of folding chairs.

Our batters pressed the Boston pitchers for four bases on balls in our half of the fourth and once we got the bases loaded we had every reason to think we could have another rally of our own. But, after Jerry Coleman walked to force Mantle home, we closed out the inning, settling for just that one run. I continued to sit quietly with the other pitchers as Tom Morgan took the mound for us in the bottom of the fourth.

While I overheard some of the guys exchange ideas on how to solve some of the opposing hitters, I took a slow, deliberate look around and tried to size up my situation. Compared to other places I had played, Fenway was enormous; the crowd was huge and awfully loud. It was like nothing I had ever seen before. This was my first big league game, and so far, I was getting to see it, first from the dugout and now from the bullpen.

Would they play me in my first game? I wondered. Surely, they must have something in mind. Otherwise, why would I have been told to go to the pen?

Morgan also found out real fast that tonight wasn't his time to shine. After one quick out, a couple of walks and an infield error, he found himself in a tight spot of his own. The chatter in the bullpen came to a hush as everyone began to wonder about who would go in next.

"We're in for a long night, boys" someone standing behind me blurted.

"Yeah, looks like Morgan left his stuff at home, too!"

At that instant the Red Sox first baseman, Mickey Vernon, smacked a whistling liner to right center for a double, chasing home two more runs and the Boston rooters turned up the volume even more. The fans loved it. The American League race was over for the year, but the Red Sox faithful were getting all the pleasure they could want by seeing their hometown heroes administer an old fashioned butt-kicking to us, the hated New York Yankees!

Had it not been for another great throw by Yogi from leftfield after a run scoring hit by Jackie Jensen, the onslaught would have continued. Lucky for us though, Berra's throw was early enough to throw out Mickey Vernon at home plate to end the inning.

Now we were trailing 9-5 as Lumpe stepped into the batters box to lead off the top of the fifth. The clamor from the stands was steady. The old stadium was about two thirds full and there was no doubt that everyone in attendance was delighted to see their team abuse Yankee pitching.

The phone in our bullpen rang just as Lumpe swung and lifted a high fly ball to Ted Williams in leftfield. One of the fellows standing nearby snatched it off the hook as Ted drifted in a few steps to make an easy catch for the first out. I tried to listen in, but it was difficult to hear what was said into the phone on our end and too brief to make much sense of it.

"Yeah ...huh? Okay, yeah...Right!"

That was it. Just a few words grunted into the receiver before it was slammed back onto the hook. No one said a word. Everyone just quietly stared in that direction and waited to hear who would be called. There was no waiting.

"Okay, Coates, get up and get loose! You're next! You're going in this inning."

This is unreal, I thought, as I stood up and stripped off my jacket. *I haven't sat down long enough to wrinkle my pants and they want me in the game!*

"You don't have much time, there's already one away!" My orders continued, "You better get moving."

Someone tossed a baseball to me as I hurried over to the pitching rubber. I slipped my glove onto my left hand and joined my hands together in front about belt level and twisted the upper half of my body from side to side. I stretched my arms upward, over my head and made a windmill motion with my right arm, just before lobbing my first pitch to the catcher.

"Oh no, my normal stretches aren't working!" I began to feel panicky. I noticed a strange numbness all over my body. For the first time I could recall, my nerves seemed to be getting the best of me. I wasn't aware of doing anything differently. I tried to increase the speed with each pitch, but my delivery motion was uncomfortable and felt awkward. My back and legs were as stiff as a preacher's collar on Sunday morning!

"Let's go, let's hurry it up!" I heard that same guy yell to me, while clapping his hands. "That's the second out!"

I sure could use a little more time, I thought. I was still as stiff as a board. What I needed was time to keep building up my speed. I needed to work my way up to my normal fastball, but time is what we didn't have. Being rushed was the last thing I needed. The pressure on me was bad enough without having to hurry.

A loud roar came up from the crowd as Mickey Mantle lined a two out single to right field. I looked away just long enough to see him turn back to the bag at first base and hope his hit would allow time for two or three more warm-up pitches. But, that was all. It was just a few seconds later when one of the guys yelled to me, "That's it, buddy, get in there, it's all yours!"

"This is crazy," I mumbled to myself. I must have had no more than about nine or ten warm up throws and now they want me to go in and face the devil himself! An unidentified hand held out my jacket for me and I grabbed it without a word. I noticed my hands were a little shaky when I poked my glove under my arm and fumbled while trying to open the latch on the bullpen gate. The last of the Red Sox players were getting near their dugout over by first base as I stepped onto the grass, making my first paces towards the mound.

"This is it," I whispered, with no one around to listen. I was all alone. A quick, prayful thought went through my mind, asking that this, the dream of a lifetime not turn into an embarrassing nightmare. The pitcher's mound seemed to be miles away. I walked on, step after step, almost needing to remind myself to put one foot in front of the other. The tightness in my legs, back and shoulders was getting more intense with each stride. *Maybe this is a dream,* I wondered. I couldn't feel my feet touching the thick grass beneath me. *I must be walking on air!*

The long walk from the bullpen seemed like it would never end. I finally made it to the infield and picked up the baseball that was left beside the mound from the last play. As I took the last big strides to get up on the hill, I recall thinking my major concern was not simply throwing the ball over the plate, but throwing the baseball towards the plate! I couldn't have been more nervous if I were walking in front of a firing squad!

A reserve from our bench had already rushed out with a catcher's mitt to catch my allotted warm up pitches. He was there to give catcher, Elston Howard, an extra moment to strap on his chest protector. My first throw skipped in the dirt in front of home plate; however, I surprised myself by hitting the mitt with the second one, even if it was a bit low. Howard came out to the plate and took the mitt from his stand-in. He pounded his bare fist into the palm a couple of times as he squatted down to take his defensive position. After he caught my final warm up, he popped up from his crouch and fired off a rocket-like throw to second base. He lifted his mask from his face and shoved it back onto the top of his cap.

"Okay, Jim!" he shouted out to the mound. "Let's get 'em!" he yelled, as he pounded his fist into the mitt one last time.

Maybe I am part of the team, I thought. *At least my catcher knows my name!*

I felt my knees quake when home plate umpire John Rice shouted, "Play ball!"

Right away, an anxious, fidgety Jimmy Piersall, the Boston centerfielder, stepped into the batter's box. I leaned forward from the waist and squinted to see Howard's signal, calling for a fastball. I nodded in agreement and rocked back, shifting my weight to my left foot. Again, I felt nothing below me. It was as if I were stepping on nothing but air! The tension in my right arm ran all the way down to my fingertips, causing me to be late releasing my first pitch. The ball sailed downward, struck the dirt and skipped past Howard on its way to the backstop. Piersall stepped away from the box and took another practice swing to ready himself for my next offering. He had watched me warm up and had obviously made note of my nervousness. He was the type of player who was always looking for an edge. He would take full advantage of any little point he could find to get on base. Piersall was always known to be a little quirky and he loved to play mind games. So, he figured he would play one of his shrewd tricks on me. Before I could complete my next windup he squared around to bunt. He laid down an excellent one, just to the third base side of the pitcher's mound. It rolled to a dead stop on the infield grass, at a spot too far in for Billy Hunter, who was playing at normal depth at third to grab and too far out for Howard to reach from his position behind the plate. Suddenly, I regained my balance and quickly moved over to my right and into position to field the ball. I snatched it up with my bare hand and got off a hurried throw to Bill Skowron at first base, just as I was about to stumble to the ground.

"Out!" was the umpire's call at first base, as my throw nabbed Piersall by a step.

"That'll teach you about trying to bunt on me!" I whispered under my breath while I watched the infielders toss the ball around the horn.

"One away!" yelled Skowron, holding up one finger and turning around to retake his place near the bag.

It was a big relief, getting that first batter out. "Now, I have some breathing room," I assured myself.

I got back on top of the mound and paused only long enough to take a deep breath, a big sigh of relief. I suddenly found it easier to move my arms and legs. I wasn't quite as rigid or tense as before. I noticed my confidence was returning after recording that first out. My breathing began to slow down, and I felt like it was time for me to take control of the situation. So much for confidence and wishful thinking!

The next batter, Ted Lepcio, Boston's second sacker, looked at a couple of my pitches which missed the plate by just an inch or two. It was his way of making me work harder and forcing me to find the strike zone on my own. It was my third or fourth pitch to him that sailed high and too far inside, hitting him on the upper portion of his left arm. That put a Red Sox runner on first and brought up their catcher, Sammy White. Another high fastball, up around the letters on his shirt was too tempting for Sammy. He swung just under the ball by the slightest touch and popped it up to the right side of the infield. This was an easy catch for Skowron, who secured it in his glove for the second out.

"With a little bit of luck, I'll be out of this inning real soon," I reasoned.

What I would need was more than just a little bit of luck!

"All I need to do now is throw strikes", I told myself. With two outs and the opposing pitcher coming to bat, I had reasons to believe that the worst part was behind me. "Just throw strikes," I repeated. This, however, was much easier said than done!

Suddenly, my control was gone! I couldn't have found home plate with a compass and a flashlight! I walked George Susce, their pitcher, as well as the next batter, Milt Bolling. Now, I would face the most potent part of their lineup beginning with shortstop, Billy Klause. Klause was a solid left-handed hitter with good speed on the bases, which qualified him to hit in the number two spot in the Boston batting order. My next mistake came when I gave him a pitch on the inside half of the plate that was located just perfectly for him to pull and that's exactly what he did! He turned quickly on that fastball, smacking a line drive, straight along the right field line and into the corner, which bounced up against the outfield wall! Before Enos Slaughter could retrieve the baseball and get a relay throw back to the infield, the bases had been cleared, three runs had scored and Klause was standing at third base with a triple!

The delirious Red Sox fans all rose to their feet. The idea that this game was meaningless for the season meant nothing to them. They all stood and cheered, enjoying the sweet taste of revenge. With my hands on my hips, I glared downward in disgust. I raked the toe of my right shoe in the dirt and stomped the pitching rubber. With a quick glance towards the dugout, I checked to see if anyone was coming out to the mound to talk to me or remove me from the game. No one was even looking in my direction.

"I'm on my own," I figured.

"Two away!" Howard shouted, standing in front of home plate. "Let's throw some strikes!"

And if things weren't bad enough, I recognized the next batter strolling to the plate. His image was unmistakable. It was the great Ted Williams himself, the "Splendid Splinter." I needed to forget about the runner on third and concentrate on my problem at home. Again, I agreed with Howard's signal that called for yet another fastball. As I started to step back into my wind up, I again felt an undeniable shaking in my knees. Looking back so many years later, I suppose it was only natural for me to react that way in such a scary predicament. As a shell-shocked rookie in my first game, I was about to go face to face with one of the greatest batters in history!

I gave it my best effort and turned loose a pretty good "heater" that stayed up high in the strike zone. Thankfully for me, it was a time for Ted Williams to show his human side, to show even he makes a rare mistake every now and then. He took a mighty cut at my offering and raised a high fly to deep right field. Williams had connected on the lower part the ball, just a bit below its center. Slaughter drifted back to the warning track and made an easy, routine catch. Finally, the third out!

I made my way slowly from the mound to the bench, where I found my jacket and grabbed a seat at the far end of the dugout. No one uttered a word to me, so I sat alone. I leaned forward and with my elbows resting on my knees, I stared down at the flattened paper cups and the tobacco juice splattered on the dugout floor. My mind was swirling, my head was spinning. I wanted a chance to slow down and reflect on what had just happened to me. But, this was not the time. This was all still too dreamlike. My solitude was broken when Jim Turner strolled over to me and placed a hand on my shoulder. "That's it, Jim," he said. "Take the rest of the night off."

The score stood at 12-5. Even though none of the five Yankee pitchers involved in this catastrophe had a good game tonight, I had hoped for a much better performance for my part. Our batters made some noise in the seventh when Skowron got a key hit, but other than that, we had very little to smile about, losing by a final of 13-7.

After the game, I managed to shower and get dressed in spite of my trance like state. I pondered the bitter disappointment I had because this game- my major league debut didn't turn out to be anything like I had dreamed. *Was this it for me?* I asked myself. *Would they want me back after a performance like this? Surely, they will give me another chance. After all, the Yankees have a lot of time and money invested in me.*

"And what about those negative, discouraging folks back home in Virginia? What will they think when they read the newspapers? Who cares? I'll do better next time, I'm sure. I've come way too far to turn back now!" I grumbled.

CHAPTER 10

The Slider

September was quickly drawing to a close, and it had been more than a week since my less than impressive debut in Boston. Despite the abuse we took on that unforgettable Friday night, we managed to recompose ourselves and win the series. We took the next two games from the Red Sox before packing up and heading south to Baltimore for a three game set.

The Yankees didn't have an easy time of it with the Orioles either. We lost two out of three at Baltimore's Memorial Stadium and showed little resemblance to the pennant winning champions we were supposed to be. After getting an 11-6 win in the middle game, we were poised to close out the series with a win in game three which would be Whitey Ford's final start of the regular season. Another victory for Whitey would make him a twenty-game winner for the year, but it just wasn't to be. It sure wasn't because he didn't do his part. Whitey pitched a brilliant game, performing well enough to have been a winner on any other day. We just weren't prepared for the clever trick Oriole manager, Paul Richards had up his sleeve. His trick was a secret weapon, one that worked even better than he had expected. Richards chose as his starting pitcher a recent roster addition, Charlie Beamon, freshly picked from the Oriole farms. At just twenty one years old, Beamon was making his first major league start, yet he pitched like a veteran headed for the Baseball Hall of Fame! His performance is what most rookies can only dream. He held the Yankees scoreless with a four-hit shutout which was sufficient to beat the Yankees and Whitey Ford 1-0! There were several pitchers scattered throughout the major leagues who won twenty games in 1956, but none on our club, the American League Champions, the team with the best win-loss record in all of baseball.

We finally made it home to Yankee Stadium for a season ending, weekend series against Boston. I was feeling as if time was running out on me. I was anxious to get another chance to pitch, yet I could easily understand why I had not been used. Recalling the nervousness and wildness I showed the previous week at Fenway Park made me doubt if they would ever call on me again.

This was my first time at Yankee Stadium and everything I had ever been told about the place was true. The atmosphere of the park itself stirred my emotions. The sense of team history and the awareness of traditions were overpowering. At that time, I wasn't quite prepared for those feelings, but years later I would look back at that moment and realize that this was the first time I was ever struck by the meaning of Yankee Spirit. Putting on the home uniform with the revered pinstripes was an awesome experience. The pride and confidence I received from all of this made me even more determined to prove myself. I really wanted another shot at those dirty Red Sox!

My wish came true. I got the call on the final day of the season. It was a Sunday afternoon game and our starting pitcher, Bob Turley, faltered in the middle innings and allowed Boston to sneak out to a 4-3 lead after eight innings. To my surprise, I was brought in to relieve lefthander Mickey McDermott at the top of the ninth inning with the outcome of the game still up for grabs. When I took the mound, I was a lot more settled than I had been in Boston. I'm sure having adequate time to warm up helped along with having the favor of the hometown fans. And this time it was different. This time I could actually feel the ground beneath my feet.

Yet again, my wildness rose to the surface causing me to quickly yield a couple of walks. However, I regained my composure with the help of some settling words from Yogi Berra, my catcher and pitching coach Jim Turner, I was able to turn things around just as quickly and avoid what could have become another sour situation. I soon found myself out of the jam. I found a way to wiggle off the hook, allowing no runs and no hits. I breathed in a giant sigh of relief and returned to the dugout. There, I received a few pats on my back from Turner and a couple of the others. We pushed across a run in the bottom of the ninth, forcing the game into extra innings and giving the New York faithful an indication that we weren't about to go down quietly.

The shadows were growing long and an autumn chill was beginning to set in when I zipped up my navy blue Yankee windbreaker and settled back on the bench. Tom Morgan was brought in from the bullpen to work the tenth for us and we soon found out that control was not his strong suit for the day. His wildness led to three walks and a bunch of base hits. Before he could get the third out, Morgan, a Yankee veteran of several seasons, had given up three runs and put us in a spot from which we would not recover.

Our regular season ended that day on a down note, and the Red Sox won 7-4 in ten innings. But, for a brief moment I could enjoy the personal satisfaction of knowing I was capable of pitching to big league batters and what's more, I had shutdown those Red Sox! As for the Yankees, I realized this game was a losing cause and no one hates to lose more than Jim Coates. Yet, that day I felt like I had settled a score, like I had paid off a little debt, one that I had owed the Boston club for the past nine days.

The National League race had come right down to the wire. It was won by the Dodgers, with just a one-game margin over the Milwaukee Braves and a two-game lead over Cincinnati. So it was a bus ride to Brooklyn for us for the opening of the World Series. Since being recalled by New York late in the year, I knew I was not eligible to play in any post-season games. However, I was told to remain with the team for the remainder of the season, but I would not be listed on the roster of active players.

"That's fine with me!" I said. There were several of us rookies in that status and while not being permitted to play, we were instructed to suit up for the games and participate in pre-game workouts. Plus, we were to be seated in the dugout along with the regulars. That's what I call a good deal!

There have been many great events in Yankee history, but few can compare to what took place at Yankee Stadium in game five of the 1956 World Series. It happened on the afternoon of October 8th with the series tied at two games each. To this point, the home team had won each of the four games and we desperately wanted to continue the trend, knowing that game six and game seven, if necessary, would be played back in Brooklyn. But, it was that day that belonged to right-handed pitcher Don Larsen, winner of eleven games for New York during the season, who made sure his name would be remembered by baseball fans for decades to come. Larsen pitched a complete, no run, no hit perfect game, retiring 27 consecutive Dodger batters! It is a special and rare occasion when any pitcher throws a no-hitter, but a perfect game is truly the experience of a lifetime. Don decided to take it a step further by accomplishing this incredible feat in a World Series game. His performance that day made him the holder of a spectacular baseball record, one that will probably never be broken. My memory of Yogi Berra jumping into the arms of Larsen, giving Don a bear hug after the final pitch is an image I will carry with me the rest of my life. What a wonderful time to be young and be a Yankee!

We went on to win the World Series, but it sure didn't come easily. We defeated the Dodgers four games to three and felt lucky to escape as winners. Bob Turley pitched ten brilliant innings for us in game six only to lose 1-0. But, in the seventh and deciding game, Johnny Kucks came through with a beautiful performance, tossing a three-hit shutout and making us the World's Champions of baseball.

The short time I spent with the Yankees at the end of the 1956 season was enough to sell me on the idea that the major leagues was where I wanted to be. I would need to find my way back. Even as a rookie, I found myself being treated like royalty, traveling first class and having the best accommodations in the finest hotels. It was a great life. It also gave me a chance to see for myself just how great it was to be a Yankee. The recognition was incredible. Everywhere we went, it seemed we were either loved or hated. But, in either case, we were the envy of everyone including the fans, the media, as well as players from the other organizations.

However, when the season ended, it was time for a reality check. Personally, I knew the reason for my late season recall, which was to pitch in mop-up situations and save the arms of the team's regular pitchers. With that in mind, I was sure to return to the minor leagues for the 1957 season. I needed to further sharpen my skills, get more experience and continue to learn my trade. I was comfortable with all of that. I knew I had a long way left to go before paying my dues. Also, I was looking forward to spending more time with my manager back in Richmond, Eddie Lopat. He had a lot left to teach me about the art of pitching and I was eager to learn. I was just a bit surprised when I found out that he wanted to get started a lot sooner than I had anticipated.

At that point in my career, my fastball was still my bread-and-butter pitch. For the most part, it had been my velocity that was responsible for getting me this far. I had developed about a half of a curveball and just a piece of a change-up, and I was in critical need of another pitch. As limited as I was, I needed another good pitch to put in my toolbox, something more, something that would keep the hitters guessing. According to Lopat, I needed to master "the slider." A slider is a unique pitch, which unlike a curveball, will tend to curve on a flat plane; whereas, a curveball usually drops as it curves. The break of a slider is not as obvious and dramatic, but it comes towards the hitter much faster than a curveball or sinkerball (as it is sometimes called). Lopat was certain that adding the slider would surely work to my advantage by increasing my arsenal of pitches. We had talked this over several times during the summer in

Richmond and I was hoping he was still anxious to resume our work.

Back then, a winter instructional league was conducted each year in the Dominican Republic. The league was comprised of many professional and former professional players, many with major league experience. They were there to develop specific skills, as I was, or were hoping to show enough talent to be offered a contract. Many of the major league clubs were involved in the program, including the Yankees, who were heavily invested with both money and players, as compared to other teams. The Yankees appointed Eddie Lopat to head their squad, and as the manager, he had considerable input as to which players were to participate. Eddie pulled the strings and saw to it that I was assigned to the team.

Eddie seemed to take me on as a pet project for the winter. He worked with me the entire season, first developing and later perfecting the much needed slider. Because of all the tireless hours he devoted to personal, one-on-one instruction with me, I was able to show significant improvement by the time the season ended. As part of my training, he designated me as one of his workhorse pitchers on that team. With my new pitch, I was much more effective, giving batters an additional pitch to look for. Eddie gave me lots of opportunities to pitch, as our team, the Dalasi Blues played out our schedule. Without being certain on the numbers, I had a pretty good season that winter. I worked quite a few innings and won quite a few games. But, even more, under the direction of Eddie Lopat, I became a more polished pitcher, more of a pitcher not just a thrower.

My time in winter ball paid off in other ways as well. The winter of 1956-57 was a time of extremely cold weather back home in Virginia. Most of the inland rivers and creeks along the Mid-Atlantic coast were frozen over. The thick ice brought much of the water traffic in the region to a standstill. Work boats sat idle, tied to the docks while the seafood industry in the area was completely shutdown. Men who earned their living by catching fish and oysters were helpless, out of work and had nothing to do but to wait for a thawing change in the weather. This harsh, frigid weather had a terrible impact on my family as well as many of our friends and neighbors. During this time, my brother Slim and his wife, Madeline, were living with Momma at her place. As a commercial fisherman, Slim had no work, leaving the household without income. Had I been at home for the off-season, like other years, I would have likely been unemployed myself, with no way to help out financially. Yet, it all seemed to work out for the best.

While I was away for the winter, the ball club covered just about all of my expenses. There really wasn't much in the Dominican Republic for me to spend my money on, as the team paid for my meals and lodging and for all travel expenses. Fortunately for all of us, I was able to send most of my salary home to my family. I definitely wasn't raking in the dough back in those days, but it was enough money to keep the home fires burning until the warmer weather of spring arrived.

It is wonderful now to reflect back on a time long ago, when we may have thought God was shutting the door on our family. He certainly appeared to be doing that in the winter of 1956. Yet, all the while, just for us, he opened a window.

CHAPTER 11

A Season on the Shelf

My time away from baseball in the winter of 1957 was a short one. After finishing the instructional season in the Dominican Republic, I was left with just a few short weeks before it was time to pack up again and head south for spring training. Of course, the time off was nice and it was great to spend time at home with my mother, but it was also satisfying, in a way, to get back to the old neighborhood where there was a handful of people who needed to be reminded of what I had been doing to earn a living the past few years.

Some of the folks in my hometown were a peculiar bunch. Maybe they were not so uncommon for a small, out of the way community and maybe not so unusual for a rural area during those years. But just the same, there were some from back home that were just plain odd in their thinking and in their attitudes towards others.

I was surprised by how some of the negative remarks and comments made by these people had stuck in my mind. At the time I signed my first pro contract, there was a small group of locals who had nothing but discouraging things to say about my chances of making a career in baseball. I heard many of the things they had to say and I seemed to recall every one of them. I was told things like, "don't waste your time" or "don't waste the Yankees' time." I was warned, "Don't bother to pack much in your suitcase, you'll be coming back home after just a few days." But it was words like those that helped teach me a valuable lesson, a lesson about jealous, resentful people. I learned how it is often the harm they try to do that strengthens another person's drive for success.

It was then that I took a look around town and noticed how these individuals were still living in the same small community, still working their same jobs, from dawn to dusk for very little pay. And many of them were waiting for the summer to come, just so they could play another season of semi-pro baseball in the Chesapeake League.

However, there was also a very positive side to the people of Lancaster County, Virginia. There was a larger following of homefolk who wanted nothing but the best for me in my new career. Among the notables of this group were some of the area's professional men. Other than my mother, these gentlemen were my biggest sources of encouragement and support. They all wanted me do well for my own benefit and also for the good of the town. "Your success would be good for the whole county," they would say.

My biggest supporters were men like John Robert Cockrell, who ran a local retail store and Mr. T. D. Marks, our local undertaker. Our local physicians, Dr. T. C. Pierce and Dr. "Jigs" Tingle, were always in my corner. It was Dr. Tingle, in particular, who remained faithful with his letters and telegrams throughout my career. He always seemed to come through with a note of congratulations when I contributed in a victory or words of encouragement when things weren't going so well. I will always be grateful for his interest and support.

It was to the delight of most of the town's people that I continued as a Yankee farmhand and returned to Richmond for another season in 1957. It was great to be assigned to a team so close to home. The location was close enough that friends from back home had no more than a ninety-minute drive to the ballpark. It was nice to find that I had my own section of rooters in the stands, people who made the trip from Lancaster to Richmond just to see their homegrown boy pitch a game. Those were the games when I wanted to do my best. I always wanted to make their trip worthwhile and make my fans from back home proud.

A few friends from home turned out for a
pre-game presentation in Richmond including
Dr. Tingle, second from left.

It was that season in Richmond that I enjoyed one of my best years in baseball. Eddie Lopat continued to work with me on my control and with further development of my slider. It was the slider, used along with my fastball, which gave me an effective combination of pitches which worked out very well. By using this "Lopat method" through the full season, I ended the year with numbers that placed me among the pitching leaders of the International League. I finished with 14 wins and 161 strikeouts. I was used exclusively as a starting pitcher and managed to keep my earned run average down, around two and a half. After the season, Eddie assured me that another call-up to New York wasn't far into the future. He was confident that my next promotion to the Yankees would likely be for keeps.

With so much hope for a bright future, I began to sense that things were starting to fall into place. As a pitcher, my career looked promising; my paychecks were a little bigger than in past years and a young girl named Ruby Sullivan was starting to take up a lot of my spare time away from the ballpark.

It wasn't long before I was seeing Ruby on a fairly regular basis. She was a working girl with a good job at the Richmond Division of the Federal Reserve Bank. I had known her for quite some time before we started dating. She would often visit relatives who were neighbors of mine back home in the tiny town of Farnham. Our relationship brought about some changes in my lifestyle which were welcomed, but a little overdue. Dating her was what it took to keep from making that long drive home to hang out with the boys night after night, as I had done the year before. All of my running around and staying out late surely took its toll on me during my '56 season in Richmond. I'm sure it had a lot to do with my disappointing record of 6 wins and 12 losses. No ballplayer can do his best when he's burning the candle at both ends. But Ruby helped me to slow down and move into a more settled, normal life. Spending time with her kept me off the highways late at night and caused me to get more of the rest I needed. As I said before, during my 1957 season with the Virginians, I was much more focused and effective and my records clearly show it.

Shortly after the baseball season ended, Ruby and I were married. My new bride and I had our own little place in Richmond, not far from her work and close to the service station where I had landed an off-season job. The station was located across the street from Parker Field, the ballpark of the Virginians, and it proved to be an interesting place for me to work. I not only pumped gasoline, cleaned windshields and checked tire pressure, but on occasions I was asked to sign autographs for motorists who drove in, recognized me as a local player and may have heard that I had spent some time with the Yankees.

With both Ruby and me working, our financial situation was going fairly well. We weren't millionaires; however, we were able to get our bills paid on time and managed to have a few dollars left over. It was late in the year that I signed on the dotted line, agreeing to buy my first new car. I had owned two other automobiles prior to this one, but they were used cars and nothing more than affordable transportation. This new one, a black and white '57 Chevrolet convertible with a V-8 motor and the optional Chevy Power Pack, was the envy of all of my friends! My first car, which I bought back in 1954, was a used '48 Chevy. To make the deal for that one, I had to walk about two or three miles from Norfolk into Virginia Beach to get to the dealer's car lot. The sales guy let me have the car for an even $100 and allowed me to finance the deal, with terms of $25 per month, only because I was a player for the local professional baseball team, the Norfolk Tars. What a deal that was. It was amazing how much I could do back then on a whopping $63.21 twice a month! As far as my salary went, things were a lot better after three more seasons in the pros.

When the spring of 1958 rolled around, I was looking forward to a year of progress, having high expectations of making even further improvements with my pitching. I carried a confidence that told me this would be the season that my career would turn the corner. I was determined to have a winning year. My control was more consistent and I was able to spot my pitches better, using all areas of the strike zone. However, in life, it is too often impossible to see the pitfalls that may lie ahead right around the corner.

After a great spring training, I again started the year with Richmond. I was a little disappointed by not going north with the big club, but encouraged that the decision to keep me on the farm wasn't finalized until the final days of camp. I had showed some of my best pitching in a few of the exhibition games around the Grapefruit League, and I knew without a doubt they would have to find a spot for me on the New York roster sooner or later.

I was off to a great start at Richmond, winning my first two decisions and demonstrating the best command of the strike zone I had ever shown. It was quickly becoming apparent that most of the hitters of the International League were overmatched by my fastball and slider. Then, out of nowhere, with a sudden, unexpected "pop" it all stopped.

As I can best recall, it was a cool night in May, during a home game at Parker Field and I was working the final inning before another small home crowd. At the split second that I released another hard slider, I heard a loud "pop" come from my right arm. It was a sound that I not only heard, but one that I felt as it seemed to pass all through my body. The pitch was a perfect one, a called third strike. However, it was a lot more to it than just another strikeout. I knew I was in trouble. The initial pain was so intense I thought a powerful electrical shock had traveled through my entire arm, from my shoulder to the tips of my fingers. Fortunately, it was the end of the game and my night on the mound was over. But the pain in my right elbow lingered on. The hot shower after the game was no help and drying off and getting dressed was a very painful ordeal. I thought about asking for help with the buttons on my shirt and with tying my shoes, yet I preferred to keep my troubles to myself.

Letting on that I may have an injury to my pitching arm was the last thing I wanted to do. The organization had lots of plans for me and a sore arm was about the worst that could happen to me, now. *Just keep quiet about it and maybe it will be okay,* I told myself. Positive thinking and self-confidence had helped me along the way many times before and I could really use some help like that now. After the game the team was leaving Richmond, going on the road for about a week and I had no intentions of being left behind because of something minor that may clear itself up in a day or two. I got my bags packed and hit the road with the rest of the guys. Wrong move on my part....

All through the night and the following day as we traveled, I could find no way to ease the pain and I could find no way to get comfortable. The team bus was no place to be in my condition. I soon found I couldn't sit, stand, sleep or even lie down. I was in misery. There was no way I could pitch if they called on me; I would be no good for anyone. So I needed to stop thinking I could hide my condition and stop thinking I was going to fool anyone. Most of all, I needed to face the truth and stop trying to fool myself.

I finally gave up and went directly to Lopat with the truth. Without any hesitation, he made my aching elbow a priority issue. In no time he was on the telephone advising the club officials of the problem. After a few phone calls, Eddie came to me with travel arrangements, sending me back to Richmond. I was set up with an appointment, to be examined by a Dr. Butterworth at the Medical College of Virginia, located downtown. Dr. Butterworth, a trusted orthopedic surgeon and specialist, was one of our team doctors, a member of the Richmond Virginians' medical staff.

X-rays taken of my right arm left no doubt about the source of my pain. Dr. Butterworth quickly detected a fractured bone in the lower region of the elbow joint, a result of extreme stress on the muscle tissue and bones of the arm, caused by pitching with such high velocity.

"This is a serious injury," the doctor confirmed. "It will never heal as it should without treatment. It is definitely serious," he continued. "But looking on the bright side of things, I don't think there is any need for surgery. With the bone properly set and a cast to immobilize the joint, you should be okay in a couple of months," he assured.

It was hard to find much to be happy about after Dr. Butterworth gave me his assessment. I followed up with his plan of treatment and soon had my right arm in a hard, plaster cast which extended from just below my shoulder to a little above my wrist. Soon my physical pain had eased, but my spirit was crushed by thoughts of what lay ahead for me. I was an emotional mess. I wondered if I would ever pitch again. I know the doctor assured me that I'd be okay. But I had a lot of doubts and questions. Would I get my fastball back? And what about my slider?

There have always been lots of horror stories about pitchers with great potential who almost made it, only to see their futures go down the drain because of sore arms. No team wants a pitcher with a bum elbow. I prayed that that wouldn't be the case for me. At just twenty-five years old, I was horrified by the possibilities that my baseball career could slip away so quickly and my dreams would be broken forever. How could one pitch cause such a tiny fracture? How could such a tiny fracture create such a big, dark cloud of doubt to hang over my life? All of this uncertainty was frightening for me. I knew I was going to spend the balance of this season on the shelf, but what about next year and the year after that?

For the first time ever, I found myself depending on others for help with simple things which are parts of normal daily life. Getting dressed, bathing, even fixing a sandwich turned out to be a struggle with that arm of mine bound up and useless. With my wife Ruby working everyday, I thought it was best that I spend most of the summer at my mother's house. Momma stayed at home most of the time and she was always willing to give me a hand with whatever I needed.

I was in the cast for a period of about twelve weeks, beginning in the middle of May until mid-August. I was utterly miserable and totally bored. Knowing that my teammates were playing through the schedule without me only made me more anxious and uneasy. I had never had a summer away from baseball since I was a child and I definitely wouldn't want another one. The soaring temperatures and high humidity, which are parts of summer life along Virginia's coast, were really testing me. My arm was always sweaty and itchy inside the concrete-like sleeve. The cast, which was snow white at the start, turned a dingy yellow and was constantly frazzling at the edges. Sleeping was almost impossible, so I stayed in a foul, grumpy mood for weeks on end. I wanted to get back to baseball. On the pitcher's mound is where I belonged and deep inside, my heart told me so.

At last, the time came when Dr. Butterworth finally cut me free from the plaster contraption, just as I was about to turn into a mad man. What a relief it was to shed that thing! I was finally free, like a baby chick that had broken out of its shell. Now, I was curious and anxious to know more. I could hardly wait to see if I could regain my form and find my old fastball, which had been the key to my success. The minor league season was winding down with only a couple of weeks remaining, so I knew there was no time for me to get into shape and rejoin the team until the following spring. But spring was several months away and I wasn't in any frame of mind to stay idle until then. So, I came up with my own at home, off-season rehab program. I wanted to give myself every advantage possible to make a complete comeback when the opportunity came. I began a routine of exercises to help with flexibility and stretches to stimulate the muscles in my pitching arm that had been inactive for so long. I even worked with a pair of spring-loaded hand grips to strengthen my hands, wrists and forearms. I did almost everything I could think of except throw a baseball to get my body in shape. I knew it would require total commitment for me to reclaim my spot in the Yankee system. I knew I would have to prove myself to earn it back and I wasn't going to settle for anything less.

When I first met with Dr. Butterworth, he stressed with me his belief that full recovery from fractures depends upon proper treatment. He was confident that if certain broken bones are properly set, without delay and are permitted sufficient time to heal, the bones are often stronger than before the injury. That sounded good to me. But in my condition, all I could do was have faith and trust that the doctor had given me proper care and hope that his theory would apply in my case.

In March 1959, I reported to the Yankee's spring training complex in Fort Lauderdale, Florida. I arrived in camp with all the hope in the world, but with all the uncertainty and apprehension of a boy on his first day of grade school. I felt like I was facing the biggest trial of my life and I knew my future in baseball was hanging in the balance. I was cautioned to take it easy at first, to take things one step at a time. I was told the coaching staff would be watching me closely, making daily evaluations concerning my condition and the progress of my right arm. They were very careful with me, scheduling my workouts to suit a special, personalized timetable, set up just for me. At first, I was limited to a number of slow tosses, just enough to loosen my arm. Each day my workload was increased slightly by adding a few more throws. Finally, I was instructed to gradually work to build up my speed. Our team trainer, Joe Soares, kept a watchful eye on me as well. He asked to be alerted right away if I felt any pain or stiffness in my arm or shoulder. Thankfully, I had nothing to report.

After a couple of weeks, the plan seemed to be paying off and I couldn't have been more pleased with my progress. The speed of my fastball was on its way back and the sudden break on my slider was just as sharp as before. Perhaps I was on my way to making a complete comeback. Maybe Dr. Butterworth was right, maybe my arm was stronger than before. One thing was for sure, Someone Up Above was watching over me. And at this point, I had no reason to doubt that 1959 would be the season I had always hoped for.

Spring training would be ending soon, so I wouldn't have much longer to wait. I would be getting a lot of answers real soon.

In the cast from mid-May to mid-August, I was miserable.

CHAPTER 12

Mopping Up

In the early months of 1959, legendary country music star Johnny Horton saw his career take off like a rocket with the release of his historic ballad "The Battle of New Orleans." While Johnny's hit song rose to number one on the music charts, he wasn't the only one at the time who saw his career take a turn for the good. Even though I never had a rocket ride to the top or ever found the fame and riches he realized, for me, things were looking up.

Although it may not apply in baseball training camps today, it was always easy to pick out the rookie ball players from the veterans by simply checking their uniform numbers. While the player wearing number 10 was confidently working out, assured that he had a spot in the starting lineup, the young kid sporting number 70 was most likely a spring training invitee, fresh from the farm system. This was the nervous fellow who would check the team's roster to see if his name was spelled correctly.

Big Pete Sheehy, the Yankee's longtime clubhouse manager, was the sole authority when it came to issuing and maintaining all of the club's equipment, including uniforms. Big Pete apparently had access to more privileged information than most players ever realized. He did a lot more than hand out gear and inventory supplies. He had a bigger and more vital role in the day to day operation of the Yankees than most people will ever know. Pete often had the inside scoop on managerial decisions and personnel moves, long before they were put into effect. With all of his years on the job, he had acquired a sixth sense for knowing which players would be sticking with the big club, as well as those who would be returned to the minors or released. It became clear to me, even before spring workouts began, that Big Pete was in the know.

As soon as I arrived in St. Petersburg for the beginning of spring training, Pete had a little, unexpected change waiting for me. At first, I thought he was making a mistake when he was doling out pants and tops and he handed me uniform number 39. In the past I had worn 52 as a Yankee, so I questioned Pete, guessing that I may have been issued the wrong gear.

"Pete, are you sure about this? It's not the number I was given before," I asked, wanting to help the big guy avoid a mistake with his record keeping.

"No, Jim, no mistake," he responded with a slight smile. "This is your stuff."

The expression on his face caused me to believe he was eager to tell me more.

"It's time for you to get a better number," he continued in a near whisper.

There was no doubt that he wanted to keep this conversation just between the two of us.

"You should have a lower number now, since you'll be sticking with us this time."

I wasn't sure about how much stock to put into what Pete told me, but it sure sounded good. He was the team's clubhouse guy. However, he had been around long enough to have seen a lot of fellows come and go. So, for the while I was very encouraged and more excited than ever to get the season started.

Spring training was a breeze. I found no indications of pain in my pitching arm and no signs of the injury that kept me out of action for several months just a year earlier. I was kept busy throughout the exhibition schedule, pitching a lot more innings than I expected, which to me, only reinforced what Pete had predicted. Things were different now. I was part of the club, with a more active role. I was now part of their plans and it was a great feeling.

We opened the season at Yankee Stadium with a single game against the Red Sox, and like all managers, Casey Stengel wanted to put his best foot forward for the home opener. His choice for starting pitcher was Bob Turley, who had proved his worth the year before as a dependable starter, finishing with a 13-6 record. Bob sure was up for the task that day. He turned in a complete game performance and defeated Boston 3-2. His was an impressive effort to watch. The Red Sox could manage only a few scattered hits as he worked before a delighted sellout crowd of loud New York fans. He pitched as if it were mid season, showing good control of all his pitches. Casey had demonstrated a great deal of confidence in Bob and the victory proved he had made the right choice. This game, the first of the season, was a real eye opener for me. It gave me a new goal to strive towards. I wanted to work my way into position to become an opening day starter. It would require that I prove myself as a major league pitcher and earn the respect and confidence of my manager and coaches. Only then, could I be considered for that coveted first spot in the starting rotation. Of course, it would take some time, but with hard work, perseverance and faith in myself, I knew I could do it.

On the off day following the season opener, we traveled to Baltimore for a three-game set with the Orioles. Late in the first game of that series, I was brought in to relieve Don Larsen who had the Birds well in hand. For seven innings Don held the Oriole batters at bay and staked us to a big ten run lead. I worked the final two frames, pitching a scoreless eighth and ninth to earn a save. The next day, Whitey Ford started and tossed a complete game to give us a 3-1 win. What a great way to begin the season. The Yankees were sitting atop the American League standings with three wins and no losses and I was the only relief pitcher Casey had used. We had no way of knowing at the time, but our days in first place would be few.

The role of mopping up is an assignment no pitcher wants to settle for. The "mop-up" pitcher is the guy who gets most of his work coming from the bullpen into games where the outcome is pretty well decided. Often it's a thankless job, entering a game that some other pitcher has already lost. With my limited experience at the major league level, I anticipated a lot of this type of work. Rookie pitchers will often get chances to show their skills in these situations, while sparing the veteran guys from unnecessary wear and tear on their pitching arms. Mop-up duty seemed to be my primary calling for the first couple of months of the 1959 season. I was never used unless we had a safe lead or in cases where the game was a lost cause. But I was okay with the role. I was willing to pay my dues.

Simply put, the Yankee's pitching staff was out of sorts. We just didn't seem to be firing on all cylinders. With the exception of Whitey Ford and Don Larsen, the starting rotation was having its share of troubles. None of the other starters were winning consistently and no one was able to put a finger on the exact problem. Our starting pitchers were frequently knocked out of the box in the early innings which resulted in the bullpen seeing extended duty. Sometimes it was frustrating and hard to watch. Our club was struggling, playing below .500 baseball, yet we knew our talent was superior to that of any team in the majors. However, the difficulties we were incurring as a team led to opportunities for me that were completely unexpected. Our pitching troubles allowed me to see a lot more action and gain some much needed big league experience.

I was determined to make the most of the chances I was given, and by early June, I had appeared in about a dozen games and carried an earned run average of about 3.00. Both Casey and Jim Turner, our pitching coach, began to notice that I was one of their more effective relief pitchers. They agreed that the time had come for me to shoulder more of the load. They began to turn to me in some crucial game situations. For a change, I was called upon to work in spots where the outcome of the game was still up for grabs.

Corrective actions were in order for the Yankees. We could all sense that personnel moves were soon to come, as rumors in the sports columns along with clubhouse talk between players, had many of the guys on edge. The air surrounding the team was thick with tension. Our club, as a whole, was not living up to expectations -- ours or anyone else's.

The entire baseball world was shocked to see us tumble into last place in the American League in mid-May. We just weren't playing like world champions. In an attempt to patch up the hole in our sinking ship, the Yankees pulled off a big five-player deal with Kansas City, a move that would hopefully put some spark in our batting lineup as well as bolster our pitching. My old friend Jerry Lumpe, who recently had been slumping at the plate, was sent to the Athletics along with winless pitchers, Johnny Kucks and Tom Sturdivant. In return, we received infielder Hector Lopez, who had been hitting well for both power and average and pitcher Ralph Terry, a tall, young right-hander with a promising future. It sure looked like a great trade for the Yankees, but would it be enough?

By early June it became quite clear that Casey wanted more from me. In a game in New York with the score knotted at two, he summoned me in from the bullpen to face those same Athletics in the twelfth inning. I pitched two scoreless innings to take us to the bottom of the thirteenth. That's when our new guy, Hector Lopez, sliced a run scoring single to right field off our ex-teammate, Sturdivant, to give me my first win in the major leagues. It's really funny sometimes to see how player trades can work out.

It was about a week later that I earned another win. In that instance, Casey called on me to relieve Whitey Ford in the sixth inning of a tie game with Cleveland. I finished the game, yielding no runs on just one hit, pushing my record up to 2 and 0. I was showing good command of all my pitches and I was capable of throwing any of them effectively in any situation. My arm was strong, my confidence was high and I felt like I could pitch forever!

However, to this point, the season was like a bad dream for the Yankees. We were fully aware that the Indians and White Sox were steadily pulling away from us in the standings and we knew they were the two teams we needed to beat if we were to get back into the race. That's what made a mid-season doubleheader in Yankee Stadium so difficult for me to accept. It was in the fourteenth inning of the nightcap, that I surrendered a solo homerun to Cleveland's first baseman, Vic Power. The homer gave the Indians a 5-4 win and sweep of the twin-bill. It was my first loss on the year and a huge blow to my pride. I was never one who took defeat very easily and this loss to a contending team like Cleveland forced us even further behind in the standings. That gopher-ball to Power was one pitch I wish I could take back. The loss was a bitter pill for me to swallow.

As the Yankees struggled on into the sultry dog days of summer, it started to look like the Chicago White Sox were the team to lay money on. Their starting pitchers were getting the job done. The frontline guys in their rotation, Early Wynn, Bob Shaw and Billy Pierce, had dominated the league since the all-star break, giving them a firm grip on first place. We had one last September showdown with them in New York, a series that would have no impact on the pennant race. We were simply playing out the string since Chicago had all but sewn up the flag. They were ahead of the second-place Indians by several games while we were a distant third, completely out of contention. By this stage of the season, my work with the Yankees had included a few appearances as a starting pitcher, a role in which I had met with notable success. My turn in the pitching rotation led to this game, which would be my final start of the year, a match up with Early Wynn. Wynn, the grand ol' master of the game was pushing forty years old, and having one of his best seasons. After the year was concluded, he would be named the Cy Young Award winner as the best pitcher in either the American or National League. That was quite an honor, especially given the time, a period when only one such award was given annually. "Gus," as he was often called, would go on to finish 1959 with 22 wins for the season and more than 270 for his career. However, the future member of The Baseball Hall of Fame and eventual 300 game winner would come up empty on this occasion. I was fortunate to give my best performance of the year. I pitched a complete game, limiting the White Sox to just four hits and out-dueling Wynn for a 3-1 victory. It was my last start as well as my final win that season.

A season we would like to forget, 1959 was a year of disappointment and frustration for the Yankees. My rookie year was now behind me and my record of six wins and one loss is something I will always look back on with pride. Third place, however, is the wrong place to be if you're a New York Yankee. But we would be back. We were determined to finish on top next year. We were sure, because on top....that's where we belonged!

Spring training 1959; my arm felt great.
As a rookie that year,
I finished with a 6 and 1 record and a 2.88 E.R.A.

CHAPTER 13

My Sophomore Season

Since the beginning of the game of baseball, there have been many promising young players who, after completing a successful rookie season, fell victim to the dreaded "sophomore jinx." There are many examples of players who hit the ground running when they landed in the major leagues, then disappeared from the scene as quickly as they arrived. Some went as far as to earn the Rookie of the Year award following a sensational first season and were virtually never heard from again. As far as I was concerned, after my first year, I never gave it a thought. I was opening a new season, having won my last four decisions of my rookie year and I could hardly wait to get back to work. Personally, I was anxious to get the 1960 season underway and to see if I could extend my personal winning streak.

Everyone in the Yankee organization had a lot to think about during the off season. Finishing last year in third place was bad enough, but ending up fifteen games out of first place was cause for a lot of personal reflection and self-evaluation. There was a lot of work to be done. We needed to get back to doing things the Yankee way if we were to return to the World Series. My own personal goals were still in place, but they were all secondary. Team objectives came first, while all thoughts concerning individual accomplishments needed to be pushed to the back burner.

As I mentioned earlier, getting a chance to start on opening day was a goal I continued to seek. However, as I spent more time with the Yankees, I realized that most of the veteran players on the club had, at some point in their career, played in a major league all-star game. In fact, some Yankees seemed to receive all-star honors year after year and deservedly so. For many it was seen as the natural progression of being a Yankee regular.

Historically, the Yankees have long been recognized for having the capability to field an all-star caliber player at every position. With that in mind, it was no wonder that we were expected to win the championship year after year.

So I had my three personal marks of achievement laid out before me: to be starting pitcher for the season opener; to be chosen for the all-star game; and to pitch in the World Series. Setting goals is something I've always done, not just in baseball but in all areas of my life. I learned long ago that it's always best to aim high. There were many instances when I was growing up and times were tough that I had no other choice. Looking back, I can see how having lofty goals and big dreams helped me escape to a better, richer life.

Once I arrived at spring training, it was obvious that my competitive flames were burning as hot as ever. I had experienced for myself the sweetness of winning and I wasn't about to settle for anything less. From the first workouts of training camp and on through the exhibition season, I was putting maximum effort in every pitch. I didn't want anyone to hit me. This aggressive attitude and an all-out approach to pitching brought me tremendous success in the Grapefruit League games, as I had an outstanding spring that year. But at the same time, it caused me to draw complaints from some of my teammates who didn't particularly care for the way I pitched during batting practice. I just wasn't able to put limits on my competitiveness. I had developed a strong dislike for all hitters.

While this mindset did little to help endear me to some of the guys on the team, it did a lot in helping me put up the best numbers of all the Yankee pitchers in camp. At the end of spring training, I had four wins, no losses and an E.R.A. that was among the lowest in the league.

My performance was enough to catch Casey's attention and as a reward for my hard work, he chose me to be his starting pitcher for the Yankee's opening game of the regular season. His decision came as a surprise to many who thought that the honor would go to one of the more experienced members of our pitching staff. But I had proved myself with a flawless record over the final weeks of the previous season and sensational spring training. I was delighted to get the assignment, which meant I had not only accomplished one of my major career goals, but I also felt it was a vote of confidence from the Yankee brass.

It was on a sunny but chilly afternoon that I took the mound in Boston's Fenway Park for the Yankee's opener of the 1960 season. It was our first game of the new year. However, the Red Sox had lost to the Senators in Washington, D.C., the day before, in the annual Presidential opening game, an occasion that marked the last of eight consecutive seasons which President Dwight D. Eisenhower threw out the ceremonial first pitch in our national capital. But, for the Yankees, this was game one, a big day for me in Boston.

In the early innings it became a game that didn't require me to be in my best form, as I received a good amount of offensive support to assure our win. Roger Maris got his year off to a booming start by cracking two home runs, while Bill Skowron chipped in with four hits. I got in a full day's work, pitching a complete nine innings for an 8-4 win. I was allowed to work comfortably most of the afternoon as our lead over Boston was never in real jeopardy. But there was a moment in the late innings when an aging, yet still imposing Ted Williams stepped up to the plate to face me. He took a couple of practice swings, projecting a calm confidence that only a few of the game's greatest batters could show. I stood squarely, facing the plate and toeing the pitching rubber as I began a full windup. In my over-confident way, I wanted Williams to see for himself the best pitch that a cocky sophomore pitcher from the sticks of Virginia could muster.

Fortunately for me, there were no runners aboard when 'ol Teddy Ballgame connected with one of my fastballs which found its way to the upper portion of the strike zone. This linedrive, which exploded from Ted's bat, went off like a cannon! It took off, sailing directly above my head, not so high, but quickly gaining altitude. For a split second it seemed to be only slightly out of my reach, as I made a foolish and useless stab at it with my glove. Had I been able to somehow snag that speeding, low flying projectile, chances were, my left arm would have likely been taken along with it. The baseball continued to rise like a meteor on its way to straight-away centerfield. It appeared to leave the field of play in no time flat. And to my amazement, it landed several rows back in the stands for what was thankfully, just a solo homerun!

As Williams rounded the bases, I vividly recall staring down at the orange clay of Fenway's mound. I was shaking my head in disbelief. I was stunned. I had never seen a ball hit so hard, yet so low that traveled so far! Before Ted made his way to homeplate, my catcher, the great Elston Howard, slowly approached me and stopped just in front of the mound. Ellie had his mask pushed back, resting atop his navy blue cap when he reached forward to slap a fresh new baseball into the palm of my open glove.

"Don't worry 'bout that one, Jim," he advised me. "That's nothing new. Ted Williams does that to the best of 'em!"

* * *

My string of consecutive wins continued. I seemed to have no problem picking up right where I had left off the year before. The powerful bats in our daily lineup were producing runs in such abundance that it was widely agreed the job of a Yankee pitcher was the easiest job in the world. Maris, Mantle and Skowron were all hitting well and driving in runs like there was no tomorrow. Our other regulars, as well as the guys on the bench, were all contributing to our winning ways. Whenever any of our reserves were called on to fill a spot in the lineup, each of them was always up for the challenge and always did a little more than what was asked. Our batters were certainly living up to the team's old name, "Bronx Bombers."

Yet, our success was not just a result of our potent offense. Our pitching staff had the lowest E.R.A. in the league, as starters Art Ditmar and Whitey Ford were having top notch seasons. Our relievers were playing a major role in things, too. The leaders in our bullpen, relief aces Luis Arroyo and Bobby Shantz, had a real knack for performing their magic tricks in the late innings. We all had our sites set on winning the pennant this season and we were doing it with a full team effort.

By the end of June, we had taken over first place in the American League and as a team, the Yankees seemed to be firing on all cylinders. I continued my streak, racking up wins against Boston, Kansas City and Washington. A particularly memorable victory came my way in New York in the form of a rematch with Early Wynn and the White Sox. But it was against the Baltimore Orioles that I did my best work. It made no difference whether it was a home game in Yankee Stadium or on the road in Baltimore; I seemed to have the Bird's number and was able to defeat them consistently. It was especially satisfying to beat them on the road in Baltimore in front of some of my old friends from back home. There were a few folks who would often drive up from Virginia to see me pitch and it was important that they saw me at my best. I didn't want any of them to go home disappointed after their long trip.

My performances against the Orioles must have impressed Baltimore's manager, the late Paul Richards. Even today, some fifty years later, it's my old friend Ralph Terry who won't hesitate to share with anyone the flattering remarks Richards made concerning my pitching. According to Ralph, Richards once told a sports writer he would have made me his first choice if he were to pick any pitcher in the league to add to his own team. What a great compliment, coming from someone whom I continue to regard as one of the top managers of his time. But I was just as happy that Paul never got a chance to make that decision. I would have always preferred to remain a Yankee!

I was able to stay on the winning path as the summer heat of July mounted. With a perfect record of 9 and 0, I had run my streak of consecutive wins up to 13, dating back to my final four decisions of the 1959 season. I must admit, I definitely had hopes of making the all-star team as we closed in on the mid season break, the time when the selections would be announced. There was a fair amount of buzzing among the press and among some of the players about my being chosen. There was a general consensus that Al Lopez would have no choice but to pick me, since my record was the best in the league. Lopez, the White Sox skipper who had won the A.L. pennant the previous season, would be manager of the American League stars and determining which pitchers made the team was totally up to him. They were selected by the all-star manager and not voted on by the players, as was the case for starting position players during that period. Lopez had several pitchers on his own White Sox team that were worthy of serious consideration. But, like today, there were never enough places on the squad to include everyone who deserves all-star recognition. However, I had to give Lopez credit for the impartial way he handled the situation. He selected two pitchers from his own team along with Whitey Ford and me from the Yankees to join the rest of his ten man pitching staff. It's also likely that guys like Chicago's Billy Pierce and Frank Baumann, who were having great years, firmly disagreed.

As we all know, all good things must come to an end. And so it was with my winning streak. With only a couple of days left before the all-star break, I took the mound in Boston for what would be my final starting assignment before leaving the team and heading to Kansas City. The Red Sox were struggling and having a hard time picking up a win against anyone in the league. The first half of the season was drawing to a close and they were already playing under their third manager, but none of that seemed to matter at the time.

The Boston batters showed no respect for me, the newly named all-star, as I had one of my worst games in months. I was out of the game and in the showers after only two or three innings and was harshly dealt my first defeat in more than a year.

From 1959 through 1962, Major League Baseball did things a little differently when it came to all-star games. For those four years there were two contests played every July, scheduled only a few days apart. While this arrangement gave ballplayers an extra day or two off from the hectic schedule of the regular season, it also gave the members of the all-star team a little more time to meet and get to know some of the best players from the other teams around the league. The entire all-star experience was an exciting time for me. It all started with the flight to Kansas City. I traveled along with Mickey, Whitey, Yogi and a few other Yankees who made the trip. Seated in the same section of our airplane was Ted Williams, who at age 41 was playing the final year of his historic career. As soon as we reached cruising altitude, Ted got up and changed seats, moving closer to Mickey and me. We had some wonderful conversations, which lasted until it was time to land. I found Ted to be a great guy to talk with when he was away from the ballpark. For the time we were together, he was just one of the guys. Incidentally, he surely knew more about playing the game of baseball and the techniques of hitting than anyone I had ever known. It was a delight to meet him and visit with him, as I found him to be very outspoken, yet pleasant and friendly. However, this same talkative, sociable guy could instantly become a holy terror, to say the least, when he was swinging a bat!

The first of the two all-star games was played at the home of the Athletics, Municipal Stadium in Kansas City. Bill Monbouquette of Boston was selected by Lopez to start for the A.L. and in spite of his nearly .500 record, he had pitched impressively for the lowly Red Sox over the first half of the season. But, once the game started, it was evident that "Monbo" had failed to pack his best pitches when preparing for the trip. The Nationals had already been handed a 5-0 lead when I was called in from the bullpen to work the top of the fourth. I managed to tiptoe my way through the powerful National League batting order, holding them scoreless for two innings. But that's not to say I was able to come away from the game unscathed. Willie Mays of the San Francisco Giants hammered one of my best fastballs to centerfield for a line drive double, which was nothing more than his way of "saying hey" and showing me who's boss! In the next frame, big Joe Adcock from the Milwaukee Braves did the same. He touched me up for another double, but he too did not get to advance beyond second base.

There was only one other N.L. batter that reached base against me that day and that was the result of one of my sliders that tailed just a little too far inside. The batter struck by that pitch was Bill Mazeroski, the Pirates' stocky second baseman who immediately headed for firstbase, uncontested. Everyone in the park could clearly see that there was nothing intentional about the pitch, yet Bill still gave me an icy glare as he tossed his bat to the side and took the base. For me, it was simply just one of those pitches that got away.

The American Leaguers put together a small rally in the late innings, but it was a case of too little, too late The Nationals got out of town with a 5-3 win. It was a tough loss for us to take, as this game was played back during the time when a lot more pride was at stake than what there seems to be for today's all-star games when current superstars often refuse to participate.

But what a great experience it was for me to play with some of the greatest players in the history of the game.

And what about Mazeroski, the crew-cut second sacker from West Virginia? Had I only been able to foresee the revenge he would take later in the year, I would have avoided hitting him at all costs.

The 1960 baseball season was still far from over.

THE AMERICAN LEAGUE OF PROFESSIONAL BASEBALL CLUBS

520 BOYLSTON STREET · BOSTON 16, MASSACHUSETTS

June 30, 1960

Mr. James A. Coates
New York Yankees
Yankee Stadium
Bronx 51, New York

Dear Jim:

Heartiest congratulations on being selected to participate in the 1960 All-Star Games. This is, indeed, a great honor and I know you appreciate the privilege bestowed upon you.

The American League office calls your attention to the fact that these games are your responsibility and should not be treated as another exhibition game; therefore, it is imperative that you fully appreciate the importance of these All-Star Games. Please stay in shape during this period and cooperate with Manager Al Lopez in every way.

Please keep this information confidential as it will not be announced to the press until July 6.

LET'S BEAT THEM!

With kindest personal regards -

Sincerely,

Joseph E. Cronin
President

JEC:br
Enclosure

Official notice from the American League President --
Some writers told me Al Lopez had to choose me for the
all-star team; I had the best record in the league.

115

FNA057 FN-NC095

1960 AUG 27 PM 12 55

CGN PD TDR NUTTSVILLE VIR 27 1034A EST

JIM COATES

  CARE NEWYORK YANKEES YANKEE STADIUM NYK

CONGRATULATIONS ON NUMBER 10 WE'VE GONE OVER THE HUMP GOOD

LUCK

  DRS PEIRCE AND TINGLE.

I could always depend on Dr. Pierce and
Dr. Tingle for support.

American League All-Star, 1960

CHAPTER 14

It Just Wasn't Meant to Be!

"It was the best of times; it was the worst of times...the season of light, the season of darkness." These words, the opening lines from *A Tale of Two Cities,* were penned by Charles Dickens more than a century ago, yet they seem to sum things up precisely whenever I reflect on my second full season in the major leagues, the season of 1960. For me it was definitely a year of highs and lows, of ups and downs and a season of streaks. I began the baseball year by rolling off nine more consecutive wins for the Yankees and ending the regular season with four more. However, it was what took place in between as well as a most heartbreaking post-season that I would just as soon forget.

The second all-star game of 1960 was another disappointment for the American League. The Nationals triumphed again in this one by a 6-0 score. N.L. pitchers, led by Vernon Law of the Pirates and Johnny Podres of Los Angeles, kept our hitters off balance all afternoon. They did an incredible job of shutting down our powerful line-up and not permitting us to score throughout the full nine innings. Their batters seemed to make themselves at home that day in Yankee Stadium, pounding out one hit after another, including a couple of long homeruns by Willie Mays and Stan Musial. It was just as well that I had no part in this lopsided affair, other than offering a tip of my cap during the player introductions prior to the game.

Following the all-star break, I found it difficult to get back to my winning ways. My first two starts were disastrous. I resumed the season by suffering the loss in a 12-0 whitewashing at the hands of the Detroit Tigers in a home game at Yankee Stadium. It was the kind of day where I would have been better off if I had stayed in bed. I had nothing on my pitches and the Tigers took full advantage of my ineffectiveness. For two miserable innings, I floundered on the mound, searching for a pitch, any pitch, that would work, before Casey Stengel came for me with the hook. I hated to lose to any team in the league, but it was especially hard to take whenever I lost to Detroit.

The Yankees and Tigers have maintained a fierce and sometimes bitter rivalry, which dates back to the early part of the twentieth century. It is well documented how quickly the two clubs could reach the boiling point back during the days when Babe Ruth and Ty Cobb went head to head. So I was not the only Yankee to ever harbor harsh feelings of disdain toward the Tigers. Yet, by the same token, my personal sore spot with that team was because of one player in particular, their first baseman, Norm Cash. He was a real hotdog!

Now, I will readily admit that Cash was one of the best left-handed hitters in all of baseball, but it was his physical manner and body language that clearly showed his craving for attention exceeded his exceptional talents. Surely, he knew his irritating ways were getting under my skin, so I held nothing back whenever he stepped up to bat against me.

Our long feud never involved verbal taunts, name calling or insults. Nevertheless, the fact that our feelings were mutual was clear to all members of both ball clubs. Whenever we squared off, it was always wise on his part to avoid digging in excessively or crowding the plate.

By early August my record had dipped to an alarming 9 and 3. I had recorded my first defeat just before the all-star break and now had a string of three straight. I wasn't yet at the point of panic, but I was totally puzzled by the sudden onset of ineffectiveness. Manager Casey Stengel and pitching coach Jim Turner were stumped as well. Neither of them had any sure fire solutions to offer. However, they both assured me that my velocity and my mechanics were fine. And, as I should have known, it would be Casey's ingenuity that helped get me straightened out.

Casey called me in his office for a private meeting, a little one on one to discuss his plan for getting me back on track. He suggested that I be taken from the starting rotation and returned to the bullpen on a trial basis, just long enough for me to regain my old form and get back in my groove.

"You did a great job for us in the past, Jim, whenever we needed a dependable reliever," Casey assured me. "And I'm sure you can do it for us again. It will be a good move for our ball club, too," he continued. "I have some other guys who need to get a chance at starting and if they don't do so well, I'll still have you available in the pen, in case we get ourselves in a jam."

There was little else I could do but go along with Casey's proposal. So I went about my work trying to keep the proper attitude, reminding myself that Casey said the change was for the good of the team. He inserted a few new faces into the rotation, even though our team was not in a good position in the standings to do much experimenting. Sure, we were on top of the A.L. standings, but the Orioles and White Sox were within striking distance, just a little too close for comfort. Bill Short, Eli Grba and some others received starting assignments, yet none of them were overly impressive. And as Casey had promised, he called on me numerous times for relief work and often it was in the early innings, when the game was salvageable. I was used exclusively out of the bullpen for the balance of the 1960 season, picking up four straight wins and finishing the year with record of 13 and 3.

There has been a lot both told and written over the years about the decision-making skills and the managerial talent of Casey Stengel, much of which is quite critical.

However, in the second half of the 1960 season he made some tactical moves with the Yankee pitching staff that were of great benefit to not only me personally but for the overall improvement of the team as well. Our starting corps faltered on occasions and the Ol' Professor, as Casey was often called, did a good job of changing the rotation and putting a few new arms on the mound for testing as a way to learn what other pitchers might be ready. Like any other managers, he might have made a few mistakes along the way. But I'm sure that he wasn't given his nickname by mistake.

The Yankees played like world-beaters through the month of September, finishing the schedule on an extremely high note, winning our final fifteen games in a row! We easily took the American League crown, ending the regular season eight full games ahead of the second place Baltimore Orioles. For a period of about three weeks we could do no wrong. We were red hot and we seemed to pick up additional momentum as each day passed. Everyone on the team was thrilled that we were peaking at just the ideal time. Our torrid winning streak was occurring right on schedule, at the precise point to carry us on into the World Series, or so we thought.

We were about to be cooled off by an unexpected pocket of cold weather which had formed about four hundred miles to the west of Yankee Stadium. This cold front, located within the city limits of Pittsburgh, Pennsylvania, would show itself to be powerful enough to frost over even the hot New York Yankee team, in a fashion that could not have been predicted by the best meteorologists or foreseen by the most knowledgeable of baseball experts. This frigid, cooling effect would be arriving soon, compliments of a baseball team called the Pirates.

* * *

The Pittsburgh Pirates secured the National League championship by winning 95 games and by staying a safe distance ahead of the Milwaukee Braves and St. Louis Cardinals as they crossed the finish line on October 1st. This was the first pennant for the team from the Steel City since 1927 and anyone who knows anything about that World Series will tell you, the Pirates and their fans had very little to celebrate. The powerful '27 Yankees, with a lineup known as Murderers' Row, swept the Pittsburghers in four straight games. The Yankees, with hitters like Babe Ruth, Lou Gehrig, Earle Combs and Tony Lazzeri, completely overwhelmed the underdog Pirates. So why would the Pirates be so anxious to face the new, updated version of the Yankees, who in 1960 were adequately living up to their nickname, The Bronx Bombers? The odds makers, the news media and almost everyone who was following baseball at the time agreed that New York would have no problems in making quick work of their opponents. So, as heavy favorites, every man on our ball club was confident of our chances and our abilities when we packed our bags for the first game, a Wednesday afternoon affair at Pittsburgh's Forbes' Field.

Casey Stengel was someone who had earned my trust over the years. He had done a great job as manager and had very little left to prove after we won the American League pennant in '60. The White Sox won the flag in 1959, but prior to that one season interruption the Yankees had won the A.L. title nine of the previous ten years, all of them under Casey's command. That record by itself was enough to convince me that he must have done something right. On the other hand, many folks felt that Casey had the easiest job in baseball, being a push-button manager. In fact, he did have it made when it came to selecting his lineup for each game. Barring injuries, he could have simply put the same eight batters in the same order each day and filled in the ninth spot with the next pitcher in his starting rotation. However, even considering the abundant talent he had at his disposal, Casey added a lot to the winning ways of our ball club. He gave us much more direction and focus than many other good baseball managers could have. And Casey could often heighten our confidence just by calling a quick team meeting and calmly reminding us of who we were and what it meant to be a New York Yankee. But, with just a few days to go before the World Series opener, Casey made a surprise announcement, one that would later be seen as a boulder on the tracks and cause a derailment of his career with the Yankees.

At a scheduled press conference, he let it be known that Art Ditmar was his choice for starting pitcher for game one. The announcement ignited a real buzz among the writers and had baseball fans everywhere puzzled. Ditmar, a tall right-hander from Massachusetts, had won fifteen ballgames during the year, which was tops on the Yankee staff, and for any other team he likely would have been a solid choice to open the series. That's because no other team had a southpaw like Whitey Ford.

The importance of choosing the correct pitcher for game one of a best of seven series cannot be over emphasized, for if it plays out to be a full seven game series, the man who started the first game could be used again to start game four or five. If this pitcher has worked effectively to this point, he could possibly be ready to go again in the final game after a short rest. There is no argument to say the Yankees did not have a better hand to play going into the '60 World Series or to say anyone other than Whitey was the ace of our staff. And still today it's hard not to question what could have been. What could have been if we had had the services of Whitey Ford in that series for games one, four and seven?

Roger Maris got our offense off on the right foot in game one with a first inning homer off of Pirates' starter, Vern Law, but our 1-0 lead didn't last long. Ditmar ran into serious trouble in the bottom of the first frame. It was Art's worst performance of the year, lasting only a third of an inning and getting roughed up for three runs on three hits and a walk. In serious need of some long relief help, Casey called me into the game with just one out in the first. Fortunately, my slider was sharp and I was able to get out of the spot without further damage.

When filling the role of a long reliever, the pitcher's job is to restore order and quiet down the noisy bats of the opposition, while affording his team a chance to get back into the game. Over a span of three innings, that's exactly what I did. The Yankees closed the gap to 3-2 when Bill Skowron's hit drove in a run in the fourth. With the idea that the pendulum of momentum could be swinging back to our side, I took the mound for the bottom of the inning. I wasted no time in retiring the first hitter on a lazy fly ball hit to the outfield. And then right out of nowhere, I suddenly began to find lots of trouble of my own.

I walked their third baseman, Don Hoak, on a few borderline pitches which could have been called either way, and next, with no outs, I found myself facing the Pirates' eighth place batter, Bill Mazeroski. Yes, the same Bill Mazeroski that I hit with a pitch a couple of months earlier in the all-star game in Kansas City. This scrappy second baseman had always been recognized for his exceptional glove work on defense, but not so much for swinging a potent bat. No doubt, he had memories of the sting from that inside pitch that got away from me back in July and no doubt, he saw this time at bat as an opportunity to pay me back. Ballplayers don't forget things like that, and he left me no room for mistakes when I placed a fastball up and over the middle part of the plate. He smacked the ball hard, pulling a line drive out to leftfield, a drive that had just enough distance to clear the outfield wall, sailing just to the right of the huge, elevated Longines clock....a two run homer for "Maz." And as quick as that, the Pirates are ahead with a 5-2 lead.

The margin would prove to be too much for the Yankees to overcome. In the late innings, Elston Howard chipped in with a two-run homerun of his own, which closed out the scoring for the day. The 6-4 loss ended what was a bad day for the New York Yankees. It was the first time we had tasted defeat in three weeks and this was no easy pill to swallow. On that day, we showed a batting order that could not get on track, no starting pitching and in spots, a lack of concentration. What was I thinking when I carelessly put a room service fastball over the heart of the plate... to the eighth place batter? This game was like a bad dream that we needed to put behind us. It was time to lick our wounds, patch up our pride and get ready for game two.

The next day the Yankees came out with guns a-blazing! "Bullet Bob" Turley pitched a superlative game and received more than enough run support. In spite of needing a little help from Bobby Shantz in the last inning, Turley's performance carried us for the entire game. When Shantz came into the game, only the final score was uncertain as the Bronx Bombers showed no mercy, winning 16-3.

Following a day off for traveling back to New York, Whitey Ford started game three for us before a full house of 70,000 screaming Yankee fans who would settle for nothing less than the heads of the Pittsburgh Pirates on a silver platter, and that's just about what they got that Saturday afternoon! Whitey was at his best, twirling a masterful complete game shutout. He limited Pittsburgh to just four hits for a 10-0 victory, giving the Yankees an advantage of two games to one in the series.

Huge crowds turned out again at Yankee Stadium for games four and five. However, the massive throngs of Yankee rooters would be disappointed by the inconsistent play of the home team that caused the series to take on the characteristics of a rollercoaster. The New York bats, which produced 26 runs in the second and third games fell asleep, as if some sort of mystical cruel spell had rendered them helpless. Often, a big turnout by the hometown fans and a good night's sleep in one's own bed can work wonders when ballplayers are looking for inspiration, but neither of those things seemed to help us at all. Our mighty offense, which scored more runs than any other team in the majors during the season, could muster only four during those final two home games. An impressive pitching effort by Ralph

Terry was wasted in game four, which we dropped by a score of 3-2. I closed out that game by holding the Pirates scoreless for the final two innings, but the best pitching in the world can't help when your club is not putting runs across the plate.

Game five was an even uglier affair. Art Ditmar started for the second time in the series, and once again he was unable to survive the early innings. To compound things, the Yankee batters continued to snooze. In a truly lackluster showing by the pinstripers, Pittsburgh pitchers Harvey Haddix and Elroy Face combined to allow only five hits as the Pirates took the game 5-2, thereby recapturing the lead in the series at three games to two.

Trailing in the World Series with all remaining games on the road was a predicament we never expected to be in. What's more, the news and sports reporters were still giving the Yankees a slight edge to win it all. They were expecting our heavy hitters to wake up in time to take the next two games, with the surest bet being we would win game six with Whitey Ford scheduled to pitch. Whitey wasn't about to disappoint anyone!

As predicted, Whitey did another brilliant job in Pittsburgh, his second gem of the post season. He scattered seven hits over nine innings, enroute to a 12-0 win for New York. Our big guns had erupted for an amazing 17 hits, with everyone in the batting order contributing. This awesome show of offense had put the Yankees back into the driver's seat and now, with just one game remaining, the World's Championship was ours for the taking.

The ace of the Pirates' moundsmen, Vern Law, who drew the game seven starting assignment for Pittsburgh, had already proven his value in the series by winning games one and four. His availability for the finale was the result of some tactful planning on the part of Pittsburgh's manager, Danny Murtaugh. By the same token, the Yankees had put themselves at a slight disadvantage. Our number one starter, Art Ditmar, had already made two miserable showings and was through for the year, along with our best big-game pitcher, Whitey Ford, who was responsible for two of our three victories. Yet, we were confident that we still had one more win left in us, knowing Bob Turley would be taking the hill for us. We were all pulling for him to give a repeat of his masterful game two performance here in this final showdown for all the marbles. Unlike the Pirates, the Yankee club was stacked with veterans who had World Series experience, guys who had played under extreme pressure and came out as champions. At the same time, we had no idea of what was in store or no indication that for us, it just wasn't meant to be.

Bob Turley ran into immediate trouble and required relief help from Bill Stafford after facing just one batter in the second inning. For Bill, it took very little time for him to find that he, too, wasn't the answer to the Yankee's pitching woes, and it wasn't until the bottom of the third that we found a pitcher who could throttle the Pittsburgh attack. My good buddy, Bobby Shantz, a tiny lefthander at just five feet–six inches tall, came to the mound and quickly called a halt to the uprising of the unruly Pirates. For a span of five innings he worked his magic on our opponents, keeping them scoreless and giving the Yankees a golden opportunity to get back into the game. We trailed the Pirates 4-0 when Bobby arrived on the scene, and with the help of a Bill Skowron homerun in the fifth inning and a big three-run blast by Yogi Berra in the sixth, we found ourselves leading by a score of 5-4 as we headed into the eighth.

Johnny Blanchard and Clete Boyer teamed up to drive in runs for the Yankees in the top of inning eight. The back to back hits by these guys showed that we meant business and were ready to put this matter to rest. However, with the Yankees leading 7-4 in the bottom of the inning, Shantz started to tire. By giving us superb pitching since the third inning, Bobby had single handedly afforded the Yankees all the time needed to put the game on ice. Nevertheless, he yielded a lead-off single to Pirates' pinch-hitter, Gino Cimoli, for the beginning of what would be remembered as the most painful collapse in Yankee history.

Cimoli's hit was quickly followed by what at first appeared to be an ideal infield grounder by Bill Virdon, one that could easily be converted into a rally killing double play. But, just as our sure handed shortstop, Tony Kubek, closed in on the ball, it suddenly shot upward, as if it had struck a small stone or pebble. Whatever it was, it caused the baseball to shoot off in a different, unanticipated direction, allowing Kubek no time to react and striking him directly in the throat. He dropped immediately to the orange clay of the infield, stunned, clutching his windpipe and gasping for air. Tony's infield mate, Bobby Richardson, ran to give aid to his fallen teammate, paying little attention to the Pirate base runners, which by this time were safely standing at both first and second base. As Tony slowly began to move to his feet, our trainers rushed from the dugout to provide medical assistance, followed by a slower, waddling Casey Stengel. During the long, quiet timeout, Casey watched as the trainers assessed the injury and then he had a few words of his own with Tony. As expected of a tough warrior like Tony, he insisted on remaining in the game, disregarding that he could not speak above a raspy whisper. Right away, Casey signaled to the bench for Joe DeMaestri to grab his glove and fill in for Kubek at short.

Once play resumed, Shantz surrendered still another hit; this one a single to leftfield by Dick Groat, drove in Cimoli from second, and closed the score to 7-5. I had received the call to start warming up in the bullpen at the start of the inning, so I had been given ample time to get myself loosened up. The suspension of play after the injury to Kubek provided me still more time to prepare. Stengel had seen Shantz struggle long enough and couldn't risk going any further on Bobby's weary arm. So, with runners on first and second, no outs and a run already home, I was summoned into the game to preserve a flimsy two-run lead for the Yankees. It was quite a sticky predicament to walk into, but I loved the pressure. I always wanted to be given the baseball when the game was on the line.

Game 7, 1960 World Series: Casey Stengel called on me to relieve Bobby Shantz. Casey (center) gave catcher Johnny Blanchard and me some last minute instructions.
This photo was taken just minutes before the roof caved in!

The sellout crowd at Forbes Field produced a steady roar while I made my way across the outfield grass. But I quickly tuned it out and put my concentration on the situation at hand. I finished up my allotted eight warm up pitches from the mound and paused only long enough to notice the cool autumn breeze on my face. Home plate umpire Bill Jackowski yelled, "Play ball" as he leaned forward into his hovering position behind the catcher. The batter was an anxious Bob Skinner, a tall left-handed batter with good power. However, in this situation we were anticipating that the Pirates would play it safe and not permit Skinner to swing for the fences. We guessed that one correctly. Yankee third sacker, Clete Boyer, was playing in at the cut of the grass, looking for a bunt and as expected, Skinner laid down a sacrifice bunt to the left side, right along the third base line. Boyer fielded the ball cleanly and got off a perfect throw to first in plenty of time to get the out. But the strategic move by Danny Murtaugh had succeeded. On the sacrifice play both base runners advanced a base, putting two Pirates in scoring position with only one out. Now, with first base open, there was no likelihood of a double play, which made my spot even tighter.

Rocky Nelson, Pittsburgh's clean up hitter, was next, which was a sure sign that the Yankees were far from out of the woods. Yet I was able to breathe a short sigh of relief, once I coaxed him into hitting a high, lazy fly ball to shallow right field. Roger Maris moved in and made an easy play on the pop-up for the second out. Momentarily, I had hopes of getting out of the jam without allowing any further damage. But false hopes were all I had.

There have been few players in all of baseball more beloved than Pittsburgh's great right fielder, Roberto Clemente. More than 35 years have passed since he lost his life when flying on a mercy mission to help earthquake victims in Nicaragua. Even today, he is still remembered as a tremendous baseball player and honored as a great humanitarian.

It was with two out in the bottom of the eighth inning that this future hall-of-famer came to bat and set off what would later be viewed as a crucial turning point in the 1960 World Series. The next play will always be remembered as a time of hesitation and indecision. It has been the source of criticism, blame and second guessing over the years, of which a big part should be seen as undeserved once the details of the play have been properly reviewed.

The Yankees continued to hang on to the precarious 7-5 lead when Clemente came to bat. After taking a couple of fastballs that were high and out of the strike zone, he made what looked to be an awkward, chopping type of swing at another high one. This pitch, a breaking ball, made a downward curve as it reached the plate causing Clemente to top the ball. The baseball bounced high a few feet away from the batter's box and quickly slowed down as it rolled to the right side of the infield. It traveled a path that practically split the area between the pitcher's mound and first base. Granted, it may have wandered to a point that was slightly closer to the bag at first than to me, but clearly this slow dribbler could have been scooped up by either first baseman, Bill Skowron or me. From my perspective, Clemente unintentionally placed the ball perfectly on the tiny patch of grass I will call "no-man's land." On such a play, a split-second reaction has to be made by both the pitcher and the fielder. The two players must respond to each other without a second to spare. One must field the baseball; the other must take the throw and cover the base. In this particular case, I believe the play could have been executed successfully either way. Yet, in the heat of battle, both Bill and I moved for the ball, leaving no one to cover first. Once I realized the two of us were heading for the ball, I yielded at the last second and made a frantic but needless attempt to get to the bag before the speedy runner. The play was ruled an infield single for Clemente, which pushed across another run for the Pirates.

I know all too well that there are no do-overs in baseball. However, if I were ever granted the chance to relive that play and do things differently, I would head straight for first base, take the toss from Skowron and avoid a lot of questions! To this day, I maintain that Clemente could have been put out either of two ways had we coordinated our efforts. But, like so many other things that happened that fall afternoon so long ago, it just wasn't meant to be!

The unconventional RBI single by Clemente left the Yankees clinging to the smallest of leads at 7-6. That run for Pittsburgh was a hard one to take, knowing that our defensive lapse wiped out what could have been the final out of the eighth. At this point, the inning continued since we had just violated an old fundamental rule of the game: we gave the opposition an extra out.

Catcher, Hal Smith, batting for the first time in this game was up next for the Pirates having just entered the game as a defensive replacement earlier in the inning. He was a journeyman ballplayer with several years of major league experience to his credit. Even though Smith served in the role of a backup receiver for Pittsburgh, he was always recognized for his ability to hit an occasional long ball. Pitching from the stretch position, I glanced over at first base. Seeing the runner Clemente leading away from the base with a cautious lead prompted me to clinch my teeth, simply knowing that he shouldn't even be on base. My first offering to Smith sailed high over the plate, but was too tempting for him to lay off. He made a mighty cut at the ball, missing completely for a quick strike one. Smith shook his head as he stepped back away from the batter's box. He knew he had been a bit too anxious on that first pitch and took a quick practice swing as he attempted to regain his concentration. By detecting a weakness on his part to stay away from the high one, I went back to the well again. However, my second trip to the well proved to be disastrous.

My next pitch to Smith was another high fastball, chest high and a little above the letters across his uniform. This time the results were totally different. He swung again and this time his bat connected squarely with the ball, driving it deep to left field. Back, back it carried, back and finally over the outfield wall, just above the 406 FT marker! The powerful line drive had cleared the top of the red brick wall by at least 10 or 12 feet!

I turned and stood helplessly as I watched outfielder, Yogi Berra, make a couple of half-hearted steps toward the wall before he gave up his chase. For the moment, time came to a standstill as the baseball sailed into the trees just outside of the ballpark. I was stunned! I could barely notice the dreamlike numbness that swept over my body. I could neither believe nor accept what had just happened.

Groat and Clemente had both scored ahead of Smith and were jumping in celebration as they waited for him to arrive at home plate. A sick feeling began to swell in my stomach as I saw Casey slowly ambling, making his way to the mound. My day was finished; he was taking me out of the game.

The Yankee's parade of pitchers continued. Ralph Terry, our fifth hurler for the game was called on to replace me, inheriting a bases empty situation with two outs. But, unfortunately for the New York Yankees, it was a whole new ballgame; the Pirates had grabbed the lead, 9-7!

I hung my head as I walked slowly to the bench, upset with myself and realizing I had no one else to blame. I felt mad enough to punch a hole in the dugout wall, but I managed to keep a lid on my emotions, as I surely didn't want to make matters worse by doing something stupid, especially on national television. Yet, all the while, I felt solely responsible for so much of what had happened. I couldn't bring myself to look at the faces of any of my teammates, so I angrily snatched up my jacket and without a word, headed for the passageway to the clubhouse. I couldn't bear to hang around and watch anymore.

Nevertheless, the game was far from over. The Yankee batters came out swinging again in the top of the ninth inning. They showed once again the positive, never-give-up mindset which has played such a vital part in the team's unmatched success. It was that Yankee Pride that came to the surface once again in our final time at bat.

Bobby Richardson and Dale Long led off the inning with singles, followed by a timely run-scoring hit by Mickey Mantle. And with one out, Yogi chased home another run to tie the score when he slashed a hard grounder to first base and was retired unassisted. The game was tied at 9 as we moved on the last of the ninth. The Yankees had a fresh Ralph Terry returning to the mound, while Pittsburgh would be sending their eighth, ninth and lead-off hitters up to the plate. Not a bad scenario for the Yankees, right? It looked like another time at bat was ours for the taking. But once again, it just wasn't meant to be.

The first guy up to bat in the home half of the ninth was second baseman, Bill Mazeroski. Not known as a power hitter or a clutch performer with the bat, Mazeroski had still been an irritating thorn in my side going back to the all-star game in July. I'm sure he was never going to forget being hit by one of my sliders, but I thought he had already inflicted his revenge earlier in the series when he touched me up for a home run in game one. It was that homer that drove in what would be the winning run for Pittsburgh in the opener. But it was on this most unlucky day, October 13th, which he would show the Yankees that he wasn't finished with us yet.

Mazeroski's turn at bat to start the bottom of the ninth will always be remembered as one of the darkest moments in Yankee history, a bitter recollection for players and fans alike for decades to come. It was Ralph Terry's second pitch to Maz that ended it all, driving the final nail in the Yankee's coffin for 1960. It was that second pitch from Terry, which followed a warning from catcher Johnny Blanchard, urging him to keep the ball down, which found its way to the upper regions of the strike zone. Mazeroski swung and made solid contact sending the baseball on a high line drive, deep to leftfield. It continued to fly well above the vine covered wall and well above the head of outfielder Yogi Berra, who looked up, turned his back to the playing field and suddenly became just another spectator. The baseball disappeared among the tree branches just beyond the wall and eventually came to rest somewhere in the foggy underlevels of baseball history. At 3:36 P.M. that day the Pittsburgh Pirates became baseball's World Champions for the first time since 1925 when they defeated the great pitcher Walter Johnson and the Washington Senators in seven games. The city of Pittsburgh went crazy, as they should have. The fans in the Steel City had finally seen the end of their long drought without a World Series winner. At the same time, everyone in the Yankee organization was looking ahead to a long, dismal and reflective off season.

It was the last day Casey Stengel would wear a Yankee uniform. The Old Professor was fired by the team's brass about a week after the World Series for any of a number of reasons. A big mark that will always be against him was his failure to have Whitey Ford ready for a third start in the series. However, second guessing someone else's decisions is always easy to do after a loss. Some said he was let go because his age was catching up with him. Casey had turned 70 years old during the 1960 baseball season and who's to say what age is too old to be a manager? Shortly after his firing, the always personable Casey appeased the sports reporters by addressing them at an impromptu press conference. Casey calmly relayed to the writers that one of the issues that Yankee management had with his job performance was related to his age. Casey went on to say that he responded to the demeaning remark made by his employers by advising them, "I'll never make the mistake of turning 70 again!" And let there be no doubt about it, Casey was second guessed for sure. And so was I! And so was Ralph Terry!

So many years have passed now, but whenever the opportunity comes along for Ralph and me to talk, the two of us will always agree that our ongoing friendship stems from our having experienced together both the good times and the bad. We shared the joy of many victories over the years as well as this one particular day of bitter defeat. We will always acknowledge the roles we played in this time of Yankee downfall and will always be connected to each other because of it. But I can think of no better person to be connected with for any reason.

And still today, if anyone wants to ask me about the World Series of 1960, I'll just have to continue to tell them, "It just wasn't meant to be!"

CHAPTER 15

World Champions, 1961

For those of us old enough to remember, the beginning of the 1960s was an unforgettable time. It was a time of crazy new ideas and a time of change. It was also a time when portions of fear and uncertainty were blended into the mix of daily life. In 1961, the world was like a simmering pot about to boil over. Our newly elected president, John F. Kennedy, launched the U.S. backed invasion into the Bay of Pigs in Cuba, while at the same time, we were receiving government booklets, which outlined the step-by-step instructions needed to construct and furnish a fallout shelter for our family. From coast to coast Americans were scanning the skies, looking to be attacked at anytime. But we just couldn't be sure who would get us first. If the Soviet Union struck us first with their nuclear missiles, would there be anything left for those hostile space aliens who were watching our every move?

While the television news had us wondering if the entire human race was about to face extermination, a major network produced a new weekly comedy show about a talking horse named Mr. Ed. Now, if that wasn't enough to cause you to lose some part of your sanity, there was a crazy song playing constantly on the radio that wanted to know if your chewing gum was losing its flavor on the bedpost overnight!

The year of 1961 was a time of change and new ideas for the New York Yankees as well. In a move that was not well accepted initially by the baseball world, our first base coach, Ralph Houk replaced manager Casey Stengel, who was fired soon after the World Series. Much of the press felt that Casey's firing was unjustified and was nothing more than a change made for the sake of change. Some writers thought that the Yankees had more important issues to address before making a managerial switch.

When Houk took the reins of the ball club, there was no need for any player-manager introductions. He had been a part of our organization for quite a few seasons and was a true Yankee, through and through. A highly-decorated Army Ranger from World War II, Ralph played several years as a backup catcher for the Yankees. Later, he successfully managed the Denver Bears, a Yankee farm team in the American Association, before serving on Casey's coaching staff from 1955 to 1960.

Once the season began, Houk proved to be the type of manager who was easy to play for. Throughout the team he was able to instill a strong sense of pride and confidence. He had us convinced that we were still a great ball club, despite our showing against Pittsburgh in the World Series. He reminded us of our incredible winning streak at the end of the season and advised us not to dwell on any of our disappointments of 1960. Ralph made it a point to communicate with everyone on the team individually. His plan was to convey to each of us what he expected, our individual role and how each player's part would be vital to the overall success of the Yankees.

As a relief pitcher, my part in the broad scheme of things was that of a "closer." Now, keep in mind, this was long before the term took on the meaning it has today. In baseball today, a closer is usually called upon to pitch only the final inning and then only if his team has the lead. Houk's plan was to use me, along with Luis Arroyo, a short, stocky lefthander from Puerto Rico, as his late-inning relievers. We would be counted on to douse any threats and protect our lead over the final two or three innings of a tight game. It was a job that came with a lot of responsibilities, one that required that you work well in pressure-packed game situations. It was a job I would love! As I said earlier, I always wanted to be handed the baseball when the game was on the line. It was in this role that I pitched some of my best baseball during the early months of the season. With a little luck, I managed to keep my cool under fire in some crucial spots throughout May and June and earned a few saves to my credit.

The Yankees enjoyed a great season in 1961. Here I'm clowning around with Elston Howard and Mickey Mantle after a 6-1 win over the Washington Senators.

For most major league teams, spending the first half of the season in second place would be acceptable. And that is the position we found ourselves in until the dog days of late July. For four months, we made it a close race and stayed within striking distance of the first place Tigers, but that wasn't good enough for the New York Yankees. Detroit had a good club, energized offensively by the middle third of their batting order. The heart of their lineup, which was comprised of Al Kaline, Rocky Colavito and my long time nemesis, Norm Cash, was one that hit for high batting averages as well as for power. These guys all had great years in 1961, yet Detroit's pitching was also among the best in the American League. A veteran right-hander, Frank Lary, who had spent several seasons with Detroit, was another Tiger who had his finest year in '61. Lary, who was often referred to as the "Yankee Killer" since he recorded a 7 and 0 mark against New York in 1958, continued his dominance over us through the first half of the campaign. Through the remarkable performance of these all-star players and the solid efforts of many of the other Tigers, Detroit grabbed sole possession of first place at the very start of the season and remained there in the top spot until after the all-star break. That's not to imply that the Tigers didn't take a few punches along the way. I'm proud to say that the Yankees had quite a bit to do with preventing Detroit from running away with the A.L. Pennant early in the race. It was in mid-May when Detroit held about a three-game lead over us, that I experienced a personal highlight of my own, one that came along when I really needed it.

The Tigers came to Yankee stadium for a four-game weekend visit and New York fans were going crazy. They all knew this series was a great opportunity for us to make up some ground on the hated front-runners. The first game of the four-game set was played before a huge noisy crowd in the Bronx. Many of the Yankee rooters were hoping to see us break out of the ongoing spell of Frank Lary, the starting pitcher for Detroit, who always seemed to have our hitters eating out of his hand. We grabbed an early lead and held the advantage until the Tigers clawed their way back and tied the game in the late innings. Once again, Ralph Houk placed his trust in me and had me take the mound at the start of the ninth inning. The first batter I faced was Lary, an exceptional hitter when compared to most other pitchers. After working eight long innings and having only a tied game to show for his efforts, he must have thought it was time to take matters into his own hands. With one swing of his bat, he swatted a long fly ball that fell just beyond the leftfield wall for a tie breaking homerun! I couldn't believe it!

Lary's homer was all the Tigers needed to win, as the Yankees failed to score in the bottom of the ninth. The 4-3 setback was a tough loss to accept. Not only did I hate losing to Detroit, but giving up the winning hit to the opposing pitcher made it even worse. I knew I had let my team down at a time when they really needed me to be at my best.

The heartbreaker on Friday night was followed by another stinging defeat on Saturday afternoon. The Yankee batters were baffled again by Tiger pitching in an 8-3 loss. After the first two games of the home stand, the Tigers had padded their lead in the standings to about five games ahead of New York and were showing no signs of slowing down. Although it was still relatively early in the season and no time for panic, we needed to take advantage of the opportunities we had to face off against the first place club at our home ballpark. I was just hoping Ralph Houk would give me another shot at the Tigers. I needed a chance to redeem myself!

Even as a rookie manager, Houk showed that he was a man who would stick to his plan in spite of some initial disappointment. In the first game of the Sunday twin-bill, he showed that his confidence in me was unshaken when he called for me to work in another tight game situation. He summoned me from the bullpen to pitch the top of the 11th inning of an evenly played 4-4 game. With good control of all of my pitches, I mowed down the Tigers in consecutive order and hardly had time to get to the dugout and grab my jacket before the Yankee offense went to work. I watched from the bench as my teammates quickly strung together a cluster of singles to push a run across in the home half of the inning for a 5-4 win. For me, this relief appearance would give me one of the quickest wins I would ever record in my major league career.

In the nightcap game of the doubleheader, Houk called on me again when our starting pitcher, Ralph Terry, began to run out of steam in the middle innings. I was still fresh and ready to go, having barely broken a sweat in the early game. I came back to the mound with the same good velocity on my fastball and slider that I had showed just a couple of hours before. With good movement and location on all of my pitches, I handcuffed the Tiger batting order over a span of five innings for an 8-6 Yankee victory and for me, my second win of the day! The Sunday double-header sweep by the Yankees was the perfect type of rude wake-up call the arrogant Tigers deserved. They needed to be reminded that their hold on first place wasn't going to last much longer. The Yankees were about to change all of that!

* * *

By mid-summer, the Yankees were playing at full speed. We took over the top spot in the American League in late July, thanks in part to a powerful display of offense led by Mickey Mantle and Roger Maris. The "M and M Boys," as they were labeled by the news media, were getting nationwide attention as the two of them pounded out homeruns at an unprecedented rate. The entire country seemed to sense that Babe Ruth's record of 60 homers in a single season was about to fall. After all, the American League was playing a new "extended schedule" because of the addition of new teams in Washington and Los Angeles. Mickey and Roger were daily targets for mobs of sports reporters while their individual totals were mounting. They were constantly hounded, day after day, with the same questions over and over, asked by a steadily increasing number of writers. From city to city, wherever we traveled, reporters began to follow the Yankees in droves, just to get a few quick quotes from the "M and M Boys." Mickey did quite well handling all of the attention in stride. He had the type of personality to go along with the interviews and give the media exactly what they wanted. Roger, on the other hand, was private and soft-spoken. He did his best to be accommodating, yet he seemed to have constant problems with the persistent bombardment by the press. No matter how hard he tried to work with them, he always seemed to fall short on giving the right answers. Mickey was the darling of the press, while Roger withdrew and went to great lengths to avoid them. He had no desire to be part of the circus of headlines. While the two of them continued to add to their incredible homerun numbers, in turn, the threat to Ruth's mark was being taken more seriously and there were those who would do what was necessary to protect it.

At the time, baseball's commissioner, Ford Frick, who had been a close friend and associate of Babe Ruth, was not about to allow the hallowed homerun record to change hands if he could help it. So he set up an obstacle course to help safeguard his friend's old standard and to reduce the chances of anyone who may be eyeing the record. He called a press conference at his office in New York to announce the new requirements that would need to be met before any new baseball records would be recognized as official. He ruled that any new baseball record, such as the single season homerun record, would have to be set within the first 154 games of the season. Should any new record be established during the final eight games of the newly expanded 162 game schedule, that record would be noted with an asterisk to indicate that it is unqualified and not an official record. The commissioner was ready to go to any length within his power to preserve the legacy of his old friend who had passed away more than a dozen years earlier.

In September, the double-barreled assault on Ruth's record was causing even more concern as Roger and Mickey slugged away at an amazing rate, which resulted in the two

Yankee outfielders sitting at more than 50 homers each. The prevailing consensus among baseball fans and experts alike was not whether Babe's record would fall, but rather, which of the "M and M Boys" would be the one to top it.

Mantle was by far the fan's favorite in this homerun derby, but poor Mickey was forced out of action with about two weeks remaining on the schedule. He had been feeling sluggish and complained of cold and flu-like symptoms for several days before he took a friend's recommendation to visit a local New York City doctor. Following the course of his recuperated friend, Mickey agreed to receive an injection in his buttocks which was sure to have him back at full speed in just a day or two. However, this shot was what soon brought the curtain down on Mickey's season. The site of the injection became terribly infected with an enormous abscess, which forced him to be hospitalized for several days! His contention in the homerun race was over, leaving him at 54 for the year. All the while, Roger continued to endure the onslaught of reporters while inching closer to the all-time record, the record that few people, other than his Yankee teammates, wanted to see him pass.

After the Yankees had played 154 games, Roger had compiled 59 homers, which placed him at just one shy of tying the Babe. So, for the moment, the rigid and powerful Commissioner Frick could breathe a sigh of relief. In his mind everything in the baseball world was as it was supposed to be, at least for the time being.

But Roger was not yet finished. In those final eight games, he blasted two more round-trippers. It was in New York that he blasted his 61st against the Boston Red Sox in the year's final game. A new record had been established. Yet, shamefully, Roger would be denied full honors and recognition for his incredible accomplishment until six years after his death. Unfair as it was, it was not until then-commissioner, Fay Vincent, issued an edict in 1991 to have the asterisk removed from the record books. A wrong was righted and the record belonged to Roger…finally!

On September 1st, the Yankees took off on an incredible 13 game winning streak. For almost two weeks, we showed no mercy and took no prisoners. This string of wins was essentially the knockout punch we needed to deliver to eliminate Detroit from the pennant race. A Labor Day weekend three-game sweep of the Tigers at Yankee Stadium was enough to destroy any hopes they may have had of making a comeback run for first place. And what a wild three-game set it was! Mickey and Roger electrified the home crowd with each having a two-homerun game in the series. Plus, we finally found a way to defeat the "Yankee Killer," Frank Lary, solving him for only the second time that year.

Yankee fans sure had a lot to celebrate on that holiday weekend!

Over the course of our September hot streak, I added a few more wins to my personal stats, which led me to a rewarding 11 and 5 record at the season's end. However, for 1961, it was the Yankee's own "Chairman of the Board," Whitey Ford, who was the most dominate of all pitchers. Whitey finished with a brilliant 25 and 4, the finest mark in all of baseball! He was presented with the Cy Young Award, in recognition as the year's best pitcher in both the American and National Leagues. Major contributions were also made by Ralph Terry, who was 16 and 3 as well as Luis Arroyo, who worked strictly out of the bullpen to record 29 saves, a remarkable total for that era.

However, it would be incorrect to assume that pitching was the only strong suit for the '61 Yankees. In addition to the homerun numbers of Roger Maris and Mickey Mantle, the Bronx Bombers featured six power hitters who hit more than 20 homers on the year. As a team, the Yankees collectively totaled 240 homeruns, which at that point was more than any other major league club in history. By the season's end, we had won 109 games, while dropping just 53, ranking us among the best teams of all time!

We advanced to the World Series once again, but this time with a renewed spirit of determination to avenge the painful loss we experienced a year earlier. We squared off against the Cincinnati Reds who had surprised the sports world by capturing the National League title over the talent-laden Dodgers and Giants, yet the favored Yankees were forced to be on guard. With sluggers Frank Robinson and Vada Pinson in the Cincinnati lineup, we had to be ready for the unexpected. On the other hand, the Yankees offense would not be going into the World Series at full strength. Mantle was still ailing from the infected hip, while Roger Maris was both physically and emotionally exhausted following his long, grueling run at the homerun mark.

Nevertheless, our haunting remembrances of the previous World Series were unquestionably put to rest. With strong assurance, we promptly went about our work and defeated the overmatched Reds in five games. Whitey Ford did an incredible job in the two games he pitched, adding another 14 consecutive scoreless innings to his World Series totals. Whitey would eventually string together an amazing 33-2/3 innings of shutout ball in post season games, a record that would stand until surpassed by another Yankee superstar, Mariano Rivera, almost four decades later.

My only appearance during the '61 World Series was in relief of Whitey in game four in Cincinnati's Crosley Field, where I worked five scoreless innings of my own. The 7-0 victory that day did a lot more than propel the Yankees to a three games to one advantage in the Series. For me, it helped chase away the "monkey" that had been riding my back since the disastrous game seven in Pittsburgh, exactly twelve months earlier. Finally, I knew I had what it took to pitch effectively in the World Series to get the job done and to be a champion!

Being a member of the 1961 World Champion New York Yankees is the most rewarding and thrilling experience I have known. Almost a half-century has passed since those glorious days and I am still recognized for having been a part of what is arguably the greatest baseball team ever assembled. The pride and the rewards have caused me to see that the hard work, the pain and the disappointments that I endured along the way were all necessary. Each of those was a stepping stone leading me upward.

Soon after the final game of the World Series, Mickey Mantle was questioned by reporters about the greatness of the 1961 Yankees and how we stacked up in comparison to some of the other great teams of the past. In his slow Oklahoma drawl, Mickey responded to the group as they scribbled frantically in their notebooks.

"This team is just as good as any of the great ones. I can't say we're the best team ever, but there's never been a better one!"

Now, Mickey's words from long ago may still be a little hard to follow, but I fully agree. Every word is true!

In the '61 World Series, Whitey Ford and I teamed up to shutout the Cincinnati Reds 7-0 in game 4.

The 1961 World Champions celebrate: (left to right)
Bobby Richardson, me, Hector Lopez and Clete Boyer.

Yogi Berra and I are on top of the world!

CHAPTER 16

How Was I to Know?

As you can imagine, life in New York City was like a whole new world for me. There were many times I wondered just what a country hayseed from rural Virginia was doing in such a crazy city of more than seven million people! I had so much to learn when I first arrived there. There were many things, such as catching taxi cabs, shopping, finding places to eat and the huge masses of hurried, impersonal people that were all foreign to me. Now, for most of the players on our ball club, life in the Big Apple was an exciting, adventurous experience. As a rule, baseball players have always come from all walks of life. They have come from every part of our country, from the small mining towns of the Northeast, from the rural farming communities of the Midwest and from some fairly large industrialized towns and cities, and believe me, I encountered players from all of those types of places. Yet, looking back, I can't recall any others who hailed from tiny coastal communities that relied on oysters and crabs for their main means of livelihood. So initially, most of us were out of our natural element, adjusting to the new big-city lifestyle. With the exceptions of Whitey Ford and Joe Pepitone, a couple of guys who grew up in New York, we were all in the same boat. All of us had to pick up on the new routine and learn our way around town. We stuck together and we learned together. The system worked best when one of the veteran players offered some advice to assist the younger rookies, but that didn't occur often. However, experiencing life in New York together drew us closer, was great for cohesiveness and resulted in many lasting friendships.

My first place of residence in New York was the Concourse Plaza Hotel, a stately, multi-storied building on 161st Street, a very convenient location near Yankee Stadium. Considered by many as *the* place to live in New York, the hotel's elegant entrance foyer faced the ballpark, which was no more than a five-minute walk down the street. There have never been many New Yorkers who could get to work so easily.

By 1961, an ideal living arrangement came my way -- one, which for the first time allowed me to have my family live with me during baseball season. It was in Hackensack, New Jersey, that an elderly lady left her house each spring to live in Florida. This yearly routine left her house empty and available for rent until she returned in the fall. She left the house fully furnished and ready to occupy. For me, my wife Ruby, and our young children, Jimmy and Janie, ages 3 and 2, it was the perfect place. I had the house to myself at the start of the season. Then, at the end of the school year, Ruby drove up with the kids and we lived there together until September. This little place was situated just across the Hudson River from the Bronx, only a few minutes drive from Yankee Stadium, yet not in the congested heart of Manhattan. It was a steal of a deal at just $200 a month! It was a great arrangement to be with my family every day whenever the Yankees were playing a homestand and even more special to return to them after a road trip.

For me, being away on the road wasn't that bad. I didn't mind the traveling as much as some of the guys, especially if we were winning. A losing streak on the road is about as bad as it gets in the major leagues. All of the clubs enjoy the finest rooms, the best food and the most comfortable transportation available. My travels in baseball took me to so many cities and allowed me to visit and experience a myriad of things I would have missed had I been in some other line of work. I was also fortunate to have been paired with some great roommates throughout my career. While with the Yankees, I roomed with some great guys like Art Ditmar, Ryne Duren and Roland Sheldon, to mention a few. They were all great teammates and travel buddies and each of them became friends of mine for life.

In the early sixties, New York was a fantastic place to be if you were a Yankee. Of course, the guys like Whitey, Mickey and Yogi drew most of the attention, but all of us got spotted around the city from time to time. Back then, the Big Apple was crazy about baseball and the fans just loved their Yankees! We could be simply walking on the street, catching a cab, having dinner at restaurant or just picking up the laundry and often enough, we would be recognized by Yankee fans. Whether alone, with my wife or with other players, our popularity was surprising and something that most of us enjoyed…and the perks that came with all of that were great, too!

One of my favorite memories of living in New York was when the folks at CBS Television phoned me with an invitation to appear on their then-popular TV game show, "Video Village." The show was filmed in the city in their downtown studios and CBS went as far as to offer me some small compensation for my time. Naturally, I agreed to the deal, and I had a great time with a lot more fun than ever I imagined! For the game, I was teamed up with a young lady contestant who, like the other players, was an out-of-town visitor to New York. The two of us, like human tokens on a huge playing board, counted off our steps with each roll of the dice. My partner and I landed on quite a few of the prize-winning spaces as we made our way through the simulated village walkways and reached the finish before any of the others. As I recall, that young lady took home a fairly big pile of prizes in both cash and merchandise. For me, it was just great to find some other game that I could play well besides baseball!

* * *

The Yankees opened the 1962 season on a bright but blustery spring day in the Bronx before smaller than expected crowd. Those in attendance were not only treated to an opening day win over the Baltimore Orioles, but also to a special pre-game award ceremony, a very special ceremony, indeed. It was the second consecutive Yankee home opener to include a presentation of the American League's Most Valuable Player Award to our own, Roger Maris! Despite the disapproval of many Yankee fans for his assault on Babe Ruth's home run record a few months earlier, he received a warm applause from the crowd when he was presented with the beautiful ornate plaque by an obviously insincere Commissioner Frick. As expected, Roger was humble and gracious in making his brief acceptance speech; that's just the type of fellow he was. He was a wonderful person and a great friend, a modest man, who did everything with class and dignity. With all of the commissioner's efforts to prevent Roger from setting a new record still fresh in my thoughts, I found it amazing to see how an individual can so easily pat a guy on the back with one hand and stab him in the back with the other.

The American League race was a real dog fight throughout the spring of '62. The Yankees held the top spot at times in April and May, but just could not take command because of the unpredicted success of the Cleveland Indians. The Tribe seemed to come out of the gate swinging and soon found themselves as the front runners of a hotly contested scramble. In fact, heading into the Memorial Day weekend, there were only four games separating the top seven teams in the standings.

By the season's midpoint, I had built up fairly decent numbers of my own. Working strictly as a relief pitcher, I had posted five wins and only two losses, while also picking up a handful of saves along the way. I was confident that I was doing my part to help keep the Yankees in contention, while it was about this time when the league standings began to take on a new alignment.

As anticipated, the Indians began to fade and while they tumbled into the second division, the Yankees were faced by a couple of unexpected threats, posed by two of the newer clubs in the circuit: the Los Angeles Angels and the Minnesota Twins. Led by their ingenious manager, Bill Rigney, the Angels forced the sports world to stand and take notice. They suddenly became a team to be reckoned with. The Angels were winning consistently on the strength of two young power hitters, Leon Wagner and ex-Yankee, Lee Thomas. Rigney's squad also featured a trio of young starting pitchers who were making true believers of many baseball skeptics. These three, Ken McBride, Dean Chance and Bo Belinsky, all showed they were capable of shutting down some of the game's most potent offenses. On the other hand, the Twins' attack was fueled by the homerun sluggers, Harmon Killebrew and Bob Allison. This pair had a knack for smacking baseballs out of the park, no matter who was pitching. In addition, the ace of Minnesota's mound staff was veteran right-hander, Camilo Pascual. A native of Cuba, Pascual was a twenty-game winner and a perennial all-star who was regarded for possessing one of the finest curveballs ever seen. Armed with the right balance of solid hitting and effective pitching, both of these teams forced many managers around the A.L. to consume more than their normal doses of Alka-Seltzer and Tums!

That's not to say that the Yankees didn't have enough firepower to answer the call. In spite of nagging leg injuries, Mickey Mantle struggled daily, yet batted his way to another MVP season in 1962, batting .321 and leading the league in slugging average. Our outstanding second baseman, Bobby Richardson, not only fielded his position like a magician, but led the league in base hits, while Ralph Terry piled up more wins than any other American League pitcher that year with a total of 23.

By the time the dog days of summer arrived, the Yankee machine was already building up steam. The Detroit Tigers, who had been our primary adversary the previous season, had sunk to fourth place, causing us to redirect our focus on the surprising Twins and Angels who were keeping things close. The Yankees forged ahead of the pack to enjoy as much as a six-game lead in mid-August, only to find that six games is not as much of a safe margin as it may sound.

Out of the blue and with no warning, our entire team suddenly went into a slump, sending us into a six-game losing streak, our longest of the year. We began to spit-n-sputter and to break down on fundamentals. We simply weren't executing like a team of champions. And, as is often the case with any slumping ball club, the Yankees hitting, pitching and defensive play all turned sour at the same time. For a full week, as a team, the Yankees could do nothing right. Fortunately, when our tailspin finally ended, we still held an advantage of about three games over the second-placed Twins. It was quite a relief to find that we could get ourselves back on course as quickly as we did while hanging on to the league lead. After all, there was still more than a month remaining on the schedule.

I didn't see a lot of action over the final two weeks of the season as Ralph Houk used this time to test some of the younger arms on his pitching staff. It was September and the rosters of all big league teams had expanded to make room for some late season call-ups from the minors. I'm sure Houk welcomed the chance to check out a few new pitchers, especially following a particularly embarrassing loss in Chicago. In this most forgettable game, the Yankees had the White Sox on the ropes holding a 6-1 lead in the last of the ninth. With the three of us combined, Bud Daley, Marshall Bridges and I were unable to retire a single batter in that final inning, giving Chicago six runs and a 7-6 win! It must have been a ballgame such as this one that prompted my old buddy Yogi Berra to mutter,

"It ain't over 'til it's over!"

Houk, who was then in his second year as the Yankee's skipper, did a good job of keeping us focused down the final stretch and to the conclusion of the season. Under his direction, we claimed the American League pennant once again in '62, finishing five games ahead of Minnesota, sending us back to the World Series for the third time in as many years.

Before we could move on to the series, in order to determine a champion, the National League was forced to conduct a two out of three games playoff between their two West Coast entries, the Dodgers and the Giants. The two clubs had completed the season with identical records, making this short playoff series necessary. It was the powerful Giants who came out on top, a deserving team that had some tremendous hitters in their starting lineup. With superstar batters, Willie Mays and Willie McCovey, joined by Orlando Cepeda and the Alou brothers, Felipe and Matty, the San Francisco club was definitely not an opponent to be taken lightly.

Just as the media predicted, the Giants proved to be just as much as the Yankees could handle in this series which ran the maximum seven games. It was an epic battle for the crown that saw the two sides grab wins in an alternating pattern. New York was victorious in games one, three, five and seven against a stubborn squad that put up a remarkable fight all throughout the series.

At New York in game four, I faced only three batters when I was brought on to relieve Whitey Ford in the seventh inning. I was tagged with the loss for that game, which squared the series at two wins apiece. During my brief stint on the mound, I allowed two Giant runners to reach base safely before I was pulled for another Yankee reliever. Both runners, who were my responsibility, later scored on a grandslam homer by San Francisco's Chuck Hiller after I had been removed from the game. On Hiller's blast to deep rightfield, those two runners scored what would be the third and fourth Giant runs of the day in what ended as a 7-3 loss for New York.

In my only other appearance of the series, I again took over for Whitey in the middle frames of game six, played in the home of the Giants, Candlestick Park. In what turned into a rare post-season defeat for Ford, I worked several shutout innings. This 5-2 win for San Francisco knotted the games at three each and forced the final showdown the following afternoon.

For the game seven pitching match-up, Ralph Terry opposed the Giants' Jack Sanford in the series finale. The game was preceded by lots of press hoopla calling for a good, old fashioned pitcher's duel between to hurlers who had just finished spectacular seasons individually. On that gusty, West Coast afternoon, Ralph Terry turned in a pitching performance that will never be forgotten. The game will forever be remembered as the tense, nerve-wracking conclusion to one of the most exciting Fall Classics ever played.

Protecting the smallest of leads, Terry had been battling an equally impressive Sanford all afternoon long as the Yankees clung to their 1-0 lead in the last of the ninth. However, Terry had worked himself into a pickle. He had yielded a lead-off bunt single, but rebounded to fan the next two batters. The next hitter, Willie Mays blasted a line-drive double, deep into the rightfield corner, chasing the Giants lead runner, Matty Alou around to thirdbase. Had it not been for an outstanding throw from the outfield by Roger Maris which was followed up quickly by a rocket-like relay throw to homeplate by second baseman, Bobby Richardson, Alou would have likely scored the tying run. Still with two outs, but now with runners taking cautious leads from both second and third, the always dangerous, Willie McCovey came to bat with the outcome of the entire baseball season in the balance.

Ralph kept his cool in this, the most crucial, pressure packed situation a pitcher could ever imagine. A huge left-handed swinger was McCovey, who made a physically imposing image at homeplate. His reputation as a powerful, pull hitter caused the Yankee defense to play deep and a few steps around to the right. McCovey slashed a terrific, top spinning liner directly at Richardson who was positioned deep on the cut of the rightfield grass. Hardly moving an inch, he was almost bowled over by the force of the clout, but Bobby managed to corral the baseball in his glove for the final out! The shutout was complete and the New York Yankees were the champions of baseball!

I was never happier for a teammate than I was for Ralph Terry at the moment of his game seven celebration. He was lifted and carried from the field by me and a gang of several other joyous Yankees. All of us were overwhelmed by emotions, for it was Ralph who had brought us the World Title by pitching the game of a lifetime! Because of his two outstanding wins, he was voted the 1962 World Series MVP, an award that he truly needed. This accolade did so much to help soften Ralph's painful disappointment that had lingered since the Yankees' bitter loss to Pittsburgh in game seven of the 1960 series.

It had been another great year for the Yankees. This World Series title was the twentieth in the history of the franchise and this one had been the result of a genuine team effort. During the season we received steady play from rookie shortstop, Tom Tresh, who filled in after Tony Kubek was called away for military duty. For his great showing, Tom was named the A.L. Rookie of the Year. The Yankees also benefited by getting another sensational year out of Mickey Mantle. This incredibly gifted athlete continued to excel in every phase of the game while playing day after day with painful leg injuries that would have sidelined any other ballplayer. Yet, with his strong will and determination, Mick would not be denied. He garnered his third American League MVP Award in 1962, the final one he would receive during his spectacular career.

In addition, the Yankees benefited from some remarkable pitching over the course of the season. Of course, our starters were paced by Ralph Terry and Whitey Ford, who combined for 40 wins and were complemented by an improved bullpen, which was more reliable than in previous years. However, as the season was winding down, it was apparent that the Yankees had a talented crop of young pitchers that were developing quickly within our organization. Some of them were promising farmhands who were excelling at the top levels of our minor league system. Still, one or two others had already gotten the call to come to New York to start getting some work in with the big club. Jim Bouton, who had spent a big part of the '62 season with the Yankees, was already showing that he had all of the necessary tools to become a winner in the major leagues, while Al Downing, a left-handed fireballer who had been recalled from our team in Richmond, was also raising a few eyebrows. Bill Stafford, just in his early twenties, had only one year of experience with New York, yet won 14 games, and was expected to be back in '63 for an even bigger year. As for the bullpen, Hal Reniff, a stocky right-handed relief specialist, was being groomed to play a major role in the club's plans for the near future.

Despite winning another World Series Championship, maybe it was time for the Yankees to make a few changes. Some of our mainstays of the pitching staff were getting along in years at a time when there looked to be an exceptional amount of young talent appearing above the horizon. So, maybe the time had come for a passing of the torch, a time for some new blood on the team. It was a slowly changing situation to which I had never given much thought. It's just that it all crept up on me so quietly. I didn't realize the time was so close at hand.

I was only twenty-nine, still young. How was I to know I had pitched my last game for the New York Yankees?

We enjoyed our place in Hackensack, New Jersey.
Ruby and me with our two oldest, Janie and Jimmy

CHAPTER 17

You've Been Traded!

It was business as usual when the Yankees gathered for spring training in February 1963. The warm sunshine of Fort Lauderdale was a welcomed change from the cold weather that had not yet run its course back home in Virginia. In typical fashion, we played through the Grapefruit League schedule of exhibition games only to finish with a losing record. This springtime pattern had been repeated enough times during the fifties and early sixties to cause most die-hard Yankee fans to shrug it off as our deliberate way of giving other teams false hopes for the upcoming season. Nothing could have been further from the truth. Surely our loyal followers knew deep down inside that we always gave our best whenever we put on the Yankee uniform.

We opened the regular season on the road, grabbing a couple of wins from the Kansas City Athletics prior to our home opener in New York. Some significant changes had already taken place on our club which were the result of an off-season trade with the Dodgers. Bill Skowron, who had been our first sacker for what had seemed like forever, was dealt to Los Angeles in exchange for veteran right-handed pitcher Stan Williams. In recent seasons leading up to this deal, Williams had logged about 200 innings annually with the Dodgers while putting up some lofty strikeout numbers. Wanting to cash in on our newest acquisition, manager Ralph Houk inserted Stan into the starting rotation as soon as he could. The departure of Skowron opened the firstbase spot for Joe Pepitone, the youngster from Brooklyn, New

York, who had seen only part-time duty with us the year before. The Yankees were counting on Joe to add left-handed power to their batting order for years to come.

We were about two weeks into the season when we arrived in Washington, D.C., to face the Senators in a three-game weekend series and except for a couple of calls for me to start warming up in the bullpen, I had not seen any game action since the exhibition games back in Florida. Sitting in the pen game after game waiting to pitch wasn't easy for me, especially when situations came up in which I would have normally been used. To this point of the season, Houk gave most of the relief work to newcomers Hal Reniff, Jim Bouton and Bill Kunkel, who had just been acquired by the Yankees in a deal with Kansas City.

Our three-game stop in Washington concluded with a Yankee win on Sunday afternoon. We felt fortunate to have taken two of three from the Senators and were anxious to get back home to New York. It had been a frustrating trip for me because of all of the idle time I spent watching while still not having made my first pitching appearance of the season. My wife and kids and our little house in Hackensack would be just what I needed, I thought, but, the Yankees had other plans.

I had just toweled off after a quick shower and was packing my gear for the trip home when I got the word to report to Ralph Houk's office right away.

This can't be good. I haven't pitched in a game since spring training and the manager wants to talk.

"Come on in, Jim, and close the door," Houk offered as I entered the tiny office. The unusual tone of his voice was already leading me to know I wouldn't like what he was about to say. "Go ahead and have a seat," he continued.

Ralph stared down at the ashtray on his desk as he pondered his next words. He was as uneasy as I had ever seen him. The small room was silent, but for the muffled noise of some players chatting in the clubhouse and an occasional slamming of a locker door. He flicked his cigar one last time before he took in a deep breath.

"Jim, I'm sure you've noticed that we are in the process of making some changes on this club, some personnel moves…" he explained, obviously wanting to clear the way for the big bomb he was about to drop.

"Yeah, and I must be involved in one of those changes!" I snapped, cutting him off in mid-sentence.

"That's right, Jim," he went on. "You've been traded."

"What!" I blurted out. I shook my head in disbelief. "What in the world is happening?"

The office became uncomfortably quiet for a few seconds before Ralph broke the silence again.

"We have to do what we think is best for this ball club and you've been around long enough to know that trades are a big part of this business. You've done a tremendous job for us over the years," he continued matter-of-factly. "And there are other teams out there that recognize that. You are the type of experienced pitcher that is in demand throughout the league and we want to get something of quality for you in return."

Ralph was in a jam, trying to make this as soft as possible for me. Still, his worn-out pep talk just wasn't working.

"To who? When do I leave? Who did you get?" I fired back with just a few of the questions on the top of my mind.

"You're staying right here, Jim." he responded calmly. "You're going to the Senators for pitcher Steve Hamilton. All you have to do is get your gear moved over to their clubhouse. They want you and they plan to give you a lot of work and I know you'll like that." Ralph was determined, working to cushion the blow, but I was terribly upset and refused to have any part of that.

Yeah, what a load of bull! This guy is telling me how simple it all is. Just move my stuff over to their clubhouse, he says. He must think I'm pretty simple, too! What about my family and our house in New Jersey? Can we find another place here in Washington? I wondered. *Will I be able to get any of my rent money back? Who do I know on the Senators? Who is their manager?* My head was spinning. There were too many questions and not enough answers!

A professional baseball player should never be so complacent or naïve as to think he will stay with one team his entire career. That's just not the way the business operates. The deal that sent me to Washington was a clear cut, one-for-one swap of interchangeable parts. The cold hard facts of the transaction were that Steve Hamilton and I not only changed teams, we swapped lockers, uniforms, everything! He took my old spot in the Yankee bullpen, wearing my old number 39, while I was issued number 28 by the Senators, the same number used by Steve up until the time of the trade.

The sooner a player can accept the idea that he is just a piece of property that can be bought, sold or traded, the better off he will be. After all the time I had spent with the Yankee's organization I should have never had the idea that I would finish my career with them.

* * *

My transition from the Yankees to the Senators was a shocking experience. While the Yankees had a long standing reputation of operating the most successful franchise in the history of professional sports, the Washington Senators were a struggling organization in only its third year of operation. They were running on a shoestring budget and were a long way from developing a tradition of winning or a winning attitude like what I had been accustomed to in New York. It didn't take long for me to realize that I would need to undergo some major adjustments before I could get settled in my new environment.

The Washington roster was stacked with an abundance of young but untested talent which was supplemented by an assortment of aging veterans who were picked up in the expansion draft two seasons earlier. Some other expendable vets came to the Senators in other deals after having played out the better part of their careers with other teams.

The Senators' brass faced problems in almost every aspect of their operation, but they came through like winners when they hired Mickey Vernon as their field manager. He was one of the few positive forces working within the organization, but even with his exceptional knowledge and experience, he was limited in what he could accomplish with so little talent and tight financial resources. He was widely respected throughout baseball and I soon found for myself that he was one of the finest managers any player could hope to play for. Mickey possessed outstanding managerial skills and was a shrewd strategist. He did an impressive job of anticipating the moves of his opponent and was an honest and fair man who gave each of his players a chance to prove himself. In addition, he brought with him the respect and notoriety from having been on of the greatest players of his time. He had been extremely popular as an outstanding defensive first baseman and was a two time winner of the American League's batting crown. Once I got to know him well, I considered Mickey Vernon to be one of the finest gentlemen to ever walk onto a baseball field. It's a shame he didn't have more to work with when he took the helm of the new Washington Senators.

During my years with New York, all players were required to follow a strict dress code that went into effect any time the team traveled. From the time we boarded our airplane until we reached our hotel rooms, we were required to wear a business suit. In some instances the rules were relaxed a bit and we were permitted to slip by with the minimum, a sport coat and tie. But the code was strictly enforced by the coaches, whose job it was to remind us that as Yankees, we were professionals and we needed to dress like professionals. It was another old tradition the team had instituted many years ago, much like their pinstriped uniforms. These were just some of the things that helped create the classic image which the New York Yankees continue to project today.

As you can imagine, I was appalled when I was about to board the plane for my first road trip with Washington and saw my new teammates dressed like they were leaving for a picnic in the park. They were wearing blue jeans, T-shirts and some were even sporting cut-off shorts! I hadn't seen anything like that since I was in the low minor leagues. My new team would take some getting used to.

And when it came to an odd mix of characters, the Senators had quite an assortment. There were a couple of slightly built young infielders who had difficulty keeping their batting averages on par with their body weights. On the other hand, we had an aging Minnie Minoso roaming the outfield who was warned by our skipper Vernon to keep his batting helmet on for safety purposes when playing his defensive position. At forty years old, Minnie was not quite as good at judging the flight of baseballs hit in his direction as he had been during his younger days. The once fleet-footed fly-chaser of the Chicago White Sox was not much more than a shadow of his former self by the time he landed in Washington and at this point of his career, experience and leadership were about all he had to offer this upstart outfit.

Then there was Jimmy Piersall, the character to beat all characters. Jimmy had spent time with several American League teams, but it was as a member of the Boston Red Sox that he went to bat in Fenway Park as the first major league batter I would face in my career back in 1956. He had had an ongoing battle with mental problems and emotional issues which had made him the subject of the popular movie from the fifties, *Fear Strikes Out.* He had been involved in numerous on-field incidents which led to ejections, fights with fans, fights with other players and various stunts of outrageous behavior that only he would have pulled.

My first dealings with this guy had occurred about three years earlier when he was with the Indians. In a starting role, I had just taken the mound in Cleveland to begin the next inning and was throwing the first of my allotted eight warm up pitches when I was suddenly distracted by Piersall, the next scheduled hitter. He was swinging a couple of bats, while standing near the playing field, just outside the thirdbase line and nowhere close to the Indians' on-deck circle. He began to purposely time his swings with each pitch as I delivered the baseball towards homeplate. Sure, he wanted to adjust the timing of his batting stoke to suit the speed of my fastball, but the primary purpose of his antics was to annoy me. My manager, Casey Stengel, took note right away and yelled from the dugout, "He's not supposed to be there. Get him outta there!"

With no hesitation I followed Casey's orders and sent my next pitch sailing directly at Piersall, just about at shoulder level, catching him completely off guard. I was boiling mad and wanted to knock those bats out of his hands. Instantly, he dropped to the ground, avoiding a near decapitation! He wobbled as he tried to get back on his feet, calling me every name he could think of. To retaliate, he stooped down and snatched one of his bats up by its handle and slung it in my direction. At this point I had already stormed down from the mound and was heading straight for him, getting close enough to him to see the fiery anger in his eyes. He was enraged like no one I had ever seen! Players from both teams scurried from their dugouts, some wanting to derail the imminent fist fight while others wanted only to fan the flames. Luckily, the two of us were restrained by umpires and players and were kept apart before any punches could be thrown. I can truthfully say I had no intentions of injuring Jim; however, I was infuriated at the time and not about to let him get away with trying to interfere with the work I was given to do.

What a difference a few years can make. As a fellow member of the Senators, Jimmy Piersall was friendly towards me and a good teammate in every way. There was never any mention of our past differences, only a mutual acceptance for each other as teammates and as professional ballplayers. Yet, there would be times throughout his career when he would resume his flighty harebrained flare-ups, causing disturbances that will never be fully understood. As an opponent, he could be disruptive, a bothersome pain in the neck. But years later, anyone who ever played baseball with Jim Piersall will quickly tell you he always gave his best to the game. Too often we fail to see the burdens that others are forced to carry.

As a pro ballplayer, this was my first experience outside of the Yankee system and it required a lot of patience and flexibility. Things were really different for me as a Washington Senator, even awkward at times. Never were things more awkward than when we visited my old place of business, Yankee Stadium, a few weeks after I was traded. I was greeted warmly by the fans when I took the mound to face my former team; however, to the M and M Boys and the rest of the Yankee sluggers, I was just another pitcher for them to feast on. Roger Maris welcomed me back by pulling a long homerun to rightfield and then sheepishly running the bases with his head down while the crowd stood and cheered. I'll never know for sure, but I'd bet that my ol' buddy Roger felt a little uneasy about that one, too.

When referring to our country's first president, it has often been told he was *first in war, first in peace and first in the hearts of his countrymen.* Once when a clever Vaudeville comedian needed to spur on his audience, he delivered a laugh line at the expense of the hapless Washington baseball team, using a twisted variance of those words to describe the Senators: *First in war, first in peace and last in the American League!* The situation was still pretty much the same in 1963. Wins were hard to come by and crowds at most of the team's home games were dismal. The organization was constantly scrambling to keep its head above water financially, stretching every dollar to cover daily expenses and to meet the player's payroll. Player transactions were often made to cut salaries or to pick up needed cash for players who could attract attention from other clubs.

It was to my own benefit that I didn't allow myself to get comfortable with the Senators. My stay with that unusual mix of misfits lasted only until early July. That's when they decided that my talent was worth more to them on the player market than on the pitcher's mound. The contributions I made to the team were of no significance. I won only two games with Washington while dropping four. It seemed that all of the decisions I incurred as a Senator pitcher, both wins and losses, almost all were recorded in extra-inning games, proving that in spite of our disappointing record, we sure kept things exciting!

My contract was sold to the Cincinnati Reds, a team with a winning record that was clinging to hopes of somehow pulling off a miracle to take the National League flag. After my arrival, the Reds never posed any serious contention for the title through the remainder of the season. The best we could do was finish up in the middle of the pack, winning just a few more games than we lost. For a team that claimed to need experienced relief help at the time of my purchase, I was disappointed to find how little the Reds actually used me. Cincinnati skipper, Fred Hutchinson proved himself as a good leader and did a fine job handling his players. Yet I found whenever he made a call to his bullpen, he resorted to his usual righty-lefty combination of Al Worthington and Bill Henry. These two seasoned relief pitchers were quite a reliable pair and received the vast majority of the workload. "Hutch" had discovered a system that worked and stuck with it. Thankfully the Reds kept me active by shipping me out to their top minor league team, the San Diego Padres of the Pacific Coast League. There in the warm sunny West Coast weather I worked in about 20 games, mostly in relief and turned in a 3 and 2 record.

As a former pitching star with the Detroit Tigers, Fred Hutchinson had spent much of his life in baseball. I'm sure he had seen just about everything there was to see in the game and had dealt with player personalities of all types. But during the season of 1963 he had a brash 22-year-old rookie on his hands, the likes of which the game had never seen. This cocky kid with the flat-top haircut was Pete Rose.

He had grown up nearby in the Cincinnati area and came to the Reds as a highly touted prospect. Showing no shortage of confidence, Pete had been with the team for the first few months of the season and had already made a name for himself around the league as top offensive performer. Even then, at that young age, he was in the process of redefining the word "hustle." The self-assured rookie knew only one speed and that was wide-open and no one got to see it up close for himself more than I. As a newcomer to the Reds, I was paired up with Pete to be his roommate on the road. It would probably be more accurate if I said I roomed with his suitcase, since he spent so little time in our hotel room. It made no difference where we traveled, I saw him only for a short time after we checked in and then maybe again sometime later when he needed a couple of hours of sleep or a shower.

In a recent television documentary on the life and career of Pete Rose, his former wife told about her useless attempts to phone him at his hotel when the team was on a road trip. She described how she could almost never contact her mischievous husband because of his all-night shenanigans and also accused me of being part of the plan to cover for him. In the taped interview she questioned just how big and spacious our hotel rooms could have been. She went on to tell how she once called our room in the middle of the night and asked if Pete was there and that I responded by saying, "I don't know for sure, let me check to see." She denied ever being so simple as to believe the room was so large that I couldn't be sure if I were alone or with Pete. What the former Mrs. Rose failed to consider was how her phone call at two or three o'clock in the morning roused me from a sound sleep. The ringing telephone was quite alarming and once I finished fumbling about in the darkness and eventually found the receiver, I had no sense of time, place or maybe even my own name! I had no idea if Pete was in the room or not, sleeping in his bed or possibly in the bathroom. Honestly lady, I wasn't sure of my own whereabouts, much less those of your husband.

At the start of the 1964 season, the Reds sent me once again to their top farm club at San Diego of the P.C.L. I had no qualms with their decision. San Diego, I found was a great baseball town and a nice friendly place to earn a living.

Manager Dave Bristol ran a tight ship there and with the talent he had on that squad he kept the Padres at the top of the standings. We were an exciting team to watch with some impressive gate receipts to prove it. Tony Perez, who would go on to become a vital cog in Cincinnati's Big Red Machine of the 1970s, was our best hitter and the league's MVP for '64. Other star players on the Padres' club who were about to step up to the major leagues were first baseman Deron Johnson, outfielder Art Shamsky and second baseman Tommy Helms.

I was with a great bunch of guys and baseball was fun once again.

CHAPTER 18

Twilight Seasons

By the time a baseball player notices that his thirty-third birthday is right around the corner, he is already aware that his professional career is a lot closer to its end than it is to its beginning. He has learned all too well that nothing about his job is guaranteed and his continual employment hinges on management's whims and their *what has he done for us lately* way of doing business.

In February 1965, I reported to Al Lopez Field in Tampa, Florida, spring training home of the Cincinnati Reds and from the very start of camp I sensed that the club was not quite sure what to do with me. Not once was I told anything of the plans they had for me or the role I was to play during the upcoming season. I was satisfied with my performance during the exhibition season, yet the few times I was called upon to pitch caused me to think something was up. So, when the regular season started, it was no big surprise for me to learn that my contract was again assigned to San Diego of the PCL.

Being back in a Padre uniform certainly wasn't the worst that could happen to me. Dave Bristol was a good manager to play for and I was looking forward to getting back with some of the guys who were returning to the club from the previous year. Along with pitcher Don Rudolph, a former Washington teammate, I was referred to as one of the "old men" on the Padres' pitching staff, a label that each of us savored while the two of us surprised everyone and led the team's starting pitchers in games, strikeouts and innings pitched. But this successful left-right tandem of Rudolph and Coates lasted only until late July. Then it was time for me to hit the road.

The California Angels, who were searching for some right-handed help for their bullpen, made a pitch for me and the Reds were willing to entertain their offer. I was traded·to the Angels for pitcher Bobby Locke, who just a few seasons earlier had been a reliever and spot starter with Cleveland. But, prior to this trade, he had been contracted to the Angels' farm club in Seattle and like me, he was still trying to pitch his way back to the majors.

It took only a short time for me to find that the Angels were a top notch team, an organization that reflected the values and principles of its majority owner, Gene Autry. Yes, it was the same Gene Autry who had gained fame in movies, radio and television as *The Singing Cowboy* who had held ownership of the club since its entry into the American League in 1961. He had always been regarded as a man of his word and in just a few short years with the Angels, he had not only earned the trust of his own employees, but from practically everyone in professional baseball.

My orders from my new employer called for me to report to the Seattle Angels, the parent club's AAA affiliate in the Pacific Coast League. At first I assumed my job was simply to fill the roster spot previously held by Locke and hopefully draw a relief assignment from time to time. But skipper, Bob Lemon, the legendary Indians' pitching star was quick to let me in on the team's intentions. He claimed the Angels were placing me under his charge for what would be only a short term assignment and that I should look to get a call from the big club well before the season ends.

After less than a month of steady work out of the Seattle bullpen, the call which Lemon predicted came to pass. As a California Angel, I was finally back in the major leagues. To use the words of Mr. Autry's top hit Western song, I was *Back in the Saddle Again*!

Before I arrived in Anaheim, all hopes that the Angels had of making a late season run for the pennant had faded.

We finished the regular season in seventh place in the American League, just a scant two games behind the once mighty Yankees who had fallen on hard times. With injuries and age catching up with some of their marquee players like Mickey Mantle, Roger Maris and Elston Howard, it was sad to see my old team reduced to a second division finisher in the standings. I was starting to sense that my sentimental ties to that organization weren't going to wither up and blow away anytime soon. Maybe it was then that I first realized that I would always be a Yankee at heart.

California manager, Bill Rigney, made good use of me over those final one and a half months of the season making me one of his workhorses for late inning relief situations. I logged a 2 and 0 record and earned a handful of saves in that short span which I thought was a credible showing. However, because of the number of promising young pitchers climbing their way up the ladder in the Angels system, I found myself back in Seattle for the start of the 1966 season.

* * *

My second summer in Seattle was a most memorable one. I had a great season pitching again for Bob Lemon's squad which played winning baseball throughout the schedule and won the PCL's Western Division by a comfortable margin. Bob used me exclusively as a starter and I responded by leading the team's pitchers in wins, posting an 11-5 record. Also, for the season I led the staff in strikeouts and innings pitched, which were both notable accomplishments, considering I was recalled to California in early August.

During the weeks leading up to this promotion, my wife Ruby and I had been spending quite a bit of our time and money making preparations for a new spot on our own family roster. My wife and children had been living with me on the West Coast for most of the season and going back to the major leagues was a welcomed move. However, relocating back to the Anaheim area was a little tricky. It was no easy job for us to get everything packed in the car with two small children and another one expected to arrive any day. But, with the help of a few of my teammates and friends, we somehow got the job done. This was the built-in support system that was always present in baseball which unselfishly gave help whenever it was needed. It was a network of friends, players and their families that pitched in whenever things became difficult.

The Coates household had almost no time to settle into their new apartment in Anaheim when the anticipated big moment arrived. We had been in our new apartment only a couple of days and the Angels were finishing up a long home stand when the time came to give Ruby a speedy ride to the hospital. From the hospital entrance, she was whisked away to the delivery room while I was given a clipboard with the standard forms and paperwork. After nervously searching through my wallet and finding the elusive insurance cards, I then had to sign my name at least a dozen times before I was directed to the father's waiting room. There, I anxiously paced the floor for what seemed like hours before a doctor walked in and announced the blessed arrival. Because the team had a night game that evening, I only had a few minutes to visit with Ruby and see my new baby boy before I had to rush out of the hospital and speed to the stadium for the final game of the home series.

"How are we going to do this?" I mumbled to myself as I darted in and out of traffic. "We will finish the home stand with Minnesota tonight and leave immediately after the game on a flight to Chicago. Ruby is still in the hospital and Jimmy and Janie are staying with neighbors. I can't just leave my family at a time like this!" Once again, it was caring, supportive friends who came to our rescue.

By the time I finally made it to the Angels' clubhouse, the look of concern and worry must have been all over my face. Without a word, I headed straight to my locker, sat on the tall wooden stool and started to unbutton my shirt when a young buddy of mine, pitcher Jim McGlothlin, whose locker was nearby, walked over to me and for a few seconds just stood and stared.

"What's going on, Jim?" he asked. "Are you okay? You look like you're in some kind of trouble. How is Ruby? Has the baby arrived yet?"

This guy was reading me like a book. It only took him one quick look and he saw that I was worried and anxious about something. He had already finished dressing and was standing there in his white Angels' home uniform waiting for answers. He was ready to take the field, yet I could tell he wasn't about to budge until he got a response.

"Yeah, thanks Jim, the baby's here," I announced. "I just left the hospital a few minutes ago and both Ruby and our new son are doing just fine."

"Well, congratulations, Jim, congratulations to both of you!" he beamed as his freckled face broke into a wide smile. He reached out and grabbed my right hand and gave it a hearty shake.

"I'm very happy for you. But, what's wrong? Something's eating at you, for sure," he persisted.

Not sure how deep to go into my dilemma, I decided to start with just some sketchy details. I knew "Red" pretty well, having played with him the past two seasons in Seattle. As a roommate, he had been one of my favorites and I found him to be a great kid, very friendly and outgoing. But I was still hesitant to burden him with my family problems.

"Well, it's like this," I began. "We leave for Chicago when tonight's game is over and we'll be on the road for the next two weeks. Ruby is in the hospital with the baby and our kids, Jimmy and Janie, are staying with neighbors. We just arrived in town a few days ago and everything has happened so fast we didn't get to make any arrangements. All of this has come on us at a bad time. I suppose I should go to the team office or maybe I should get on the phone and find someone who can give us a hand until I get back."

"No way, Jim!" he snapped back. "There's no need for any of that."

Suddenly this easy-going 22-year-old was stepping up and taking charge. "I'm calling my wife Janice right now and I'll explain the whole story to her. I know she'll be happy to go to the hospital and check on Ruby from time to time. We'll also be pleased to have your kids stay at our place until Ruby returns home and gets back on her feet."

Before I had time to respond to the offer, Jim was on his way to the clubhouse phone. Simply put, he just wasn't going to take no for an answer. Moments later he slowly sauntered back towards my locker.

"Well, Jim, it's all taken care of," he reported. "I just explained the whole situation to Janice. We have lots of extra space at our place and we're happy to help you guys out for the next couple of weeks. Now let's get outta here. We have a game to play!"

That evening I spent the entire game riding the bench, watching from the dugout. It had been a hectic, demanding day so it was great to have the night off. It had been a special day for me as both a father and a husband, so naturally my thoughts were, at times, with my wife and new baby boy. I felt relieved knowing my family wouldn't be alone while I was away and confident she would be well cared for. During the seventh inning stretch, a special message appeared on the electronic scoreboard high above the outfield wall:

AN ANGEL HALO!
ANGEL PITCHER JIM COATES BECAME
THE FATHER OF 8LB SON TODAY.
BOTH MRS. COATES AND MICKEY CHARLES
DOING FINE.

Applause came up from the already standing crowd and a few thoughtful teammates walked over to give me a friendly pat on the back or a quick handshake to just make the moment even more special.

Welcome to the world, Mickey, I thought wishfully as I stared again out towards the message board. *I'll always want what's best for you.*

If ever greatness could come from a name, my new son was surely given that chance. After all, he was named in honor of a former teammate back in New York, a friend that I admired as much as anyone, Mickey Charles Mantle!

The young McGlothlins were a special couple who showed the real meaning of friendship. They gave of themselves when a helping hand was needed and I will be forever grateful to them. So you can easily imagine the sadness I felt when not many years later my young friend Jim "Red" McGlothlin passed away from leukemia at thirty-two years old and left behind his lovely wife Janice and three children.

* * *

My stats with California in 1966 weren't that bad. I pitched in about a dozen games with my work split evenly between the bullpen and a few starting assignments. I ended my six-week stint with the big club with a 1-1 record, which was on par for a sixth place team which crossed the finish line at two games below .500. By the same token, the Angels had shown modest improvement over the past couple of seasons and continued to retain Billy Rigney as their manager since he seemed to have his club pointed in the right direction. For some reason they hung on to me as well. They had me stay on with California to begin the 1967 campaign, my final stop in the major leagues.

I was one of Rigney's busiest firemen that season. From the early games of April until mid-August, he called on me to handle a big helping of his relief pitching. Then suddenly with no warning or fanfare, my days in the big leagues were over. I still had a few years left in that old right arm of mine and the Angels seemed to know that. I just wasn't aware at the time that I would be spending the remainder of my pro career in the PCL.

I found a new guy in charge when I got back to Seattle. Chuck Tanner, who would go on to be a highly regarded manager at the major league level, was the team's skipper and he was not finding instant success at his new position. Contrary to my pitching role with California, Tanner chose to insert me into his starting rotation for the final month of the year. The club hobbled through the balance of the schedule and was forced to settle for a spot in the lower half of the standings. My record of three wins and one loss was of no help to Chuck who was moved to another job within the Angels' system for the '68 season.

The following spring it was former Milwaukee Braves' slugger, Joe Adcock who showed up as the Seattle Angels' third new manager in as many years. Big Joe, who had worked the previous season as manager of the Cleveland Indians, was no stranger to most of the Angels' personnel since he had recently ended his playing career as California's first baseman. In addition, there were many other familiar faces around the Seattle clubhouse in 1968. There were times that year when I felt as if I were attending a reunion of Yankee pitchers from my years in New York. My old roommate, Roland Sheldon showed up there, along with Jim Bouton and Bill Stafford. And if that weren't enough to create an uncanny atmosphere, Bobby Locke, the pitcher I was traded for years earlier by Cincinnati, was there putting in time as both a starter and reliever. His determination to get back to the majors had paid off as the Angels moved him up to California and back a number of times during the late sixties.

Adcock was unable to pull any tricks that would resurrect the ball club and in spite of the rewarding year I had, the club again ended with a losing record. I went 17 and 10 on the season with an E.R.A. that ranked among the lowest in the league. I accomplished all of this while working well over 200 innings. But, as any good ballplayer will say, "It's not a satisfying season, regardless of your personal numbers, if your club doesn't win."

The Angels AAA affiliate had a whole new look for the 1969 season. The organization relocated its top farm club from Seattle to beautiful Honolulu, Hawaii, and took on the traditional name of that city's team, the Hawaii Islanders. It was a great place to live and a wonderful place to play baseball. The old rickety wooden stadium was lacking in some aspects, but the fans loved their team and filled the place almost every night for Islanders' home games. That old ballpark, situated on a small lot in downtown Honolulu was affectionately referred to as "The Termite Palace." Yet, complaints from players were few, even those from visiting teams, because the worst day in Honolulu was still better than a great day in any other city! I was fortunate to spend the final two summers of my professional career there with the Islanders and enjoyed every minute. Ruby fell in love with Hawaii and Jimmy and Janie thought they were in heaven! We had the two of them enrolled in the local public schools, which we found to be superior to other school systems. And those two kids were delighted to spend every hour away from the classroom swimming and splashing in the huge pool, which was part of our apartment complex.

Back for his second tenure as Triple-A manager for the organization, Chuck Tanner did a commendable job and led the Islanders to a respectable finish, ending with a winning slate. He depended on veteran pitchers Dennis Bennett, Bo Belinsky and me to take most of the starting jobs and we held our own with the rest of the league. Our young second baseman, Winston Llenas from the Dominican Republic, had an outstanding year at the plate. He batted over .360 and provided our club with a notable amount of offensive punch. All in all, as a team we were serving notice to the rest of the P.C.L. that we were on the verge of putting it all together.

My final season of professional baseball was 1970 and what an incredible season it was! The Islanders had an amazing year and to this day I am still proud to say that I played a part in it. Under the guidance of Chuck Tanner once again, we completed the season at an unheard of 50 games above the .500 mark and our record of 98 and 48 remains one of the most talked about finishes in all of baseball. We hit a hot streak in June, going 25 and 5 for the month. From that point on we never looked back. The club's offense was tops in the P.C.L. averaging over 5.5 runs per game and our pitching corps was exceptional as well. Dennis Bennett led the staff with 18 wins while Tom Bradley, a promising young prospect from North Carolina, went 11 and 1. Naturally at 37, I was one of the "old guys" of the league, but I felt right at home with the other pitching vets on the team. Elroy Face, Ron Kline and Juan Pizarro, who had each left his lasting mark on major league baseball, were all right there with me, contributing to the Islander's successful year.

I suppose the Angels' organization realized I was at the end of my baseball career and wanted to do it up big for my final season. We eventually dropped the league playoff series to a very talented Dodger club from Spokane which was managed by Tommy LaSorda. But for me, the loss did very little to dampen my memories of the friends, the great times and fun I had during my final year in baseball. I'm sure I'll always feel like I went out on a high note.

EPILOGUE

Since my days in baseball, the twists and turns along the path of life have been discouraging and difficult at times, while at other times, life has been rewarding and gratifying. The innings I spent on the ballfields in countless cities and towns are now just foggy memories that I will always want to hold on to. In some ways, I see that I accomplished extraordinary things which are recalled in detail by people that I have never met. In other ways, I see myself simply as someone who played a game he loved, the best he could for as long as he could.

There were times shortly after my baseball career ended when life tested me thoroughly. Sometimes I passed those tests. In other instances, I faltered, disappointed myself and fell short of what others expected from me. For me to leave the spotlight of professional baseball and grab a lunch pail and head to work each day was no easy transition. I never once received preferential treatment nor asked to be treated as someone special because of my past work. I wanted nothing more than to be one of the guys, just as it was when I was a ballplayer and just as it was when I was a teenager who chopped down trees for Chilton's excelsior mill. I deliberately pushed myself to put baseball behind me. Leaving it there took time, but I eventually settled in and became comfortable with my daily work routine.

Soon after baseball, I found a job where I literally started at the ground level and worked my way up. For a number of years my brother Slim was employed by the C.W. Wright Company, a contracting firm associated with the local electric power company. He worked on a line crew which installed overhead high-voltage lines. He somehow got the inside scoop on an upcoming position which would add another laborer to his crew. Slim used his influence and put in a good word for me which helped bring me onboard. At the beginning, my work was strictly on the ground, drilling holes and raising huge utility poles to an upright position, making them ready for installation. After months of doing the same job, I wanted to do more. I began to use my lunch breaks to familiarize myself with the gear used by the lineman. With help from Ray Davenport, Jr., an experienced yet patient lineman, I practiced climbing and picked up the proper methods for using climbing equipment and rigging. Before long I received a promotion and began working high above the ground, stringing new lines and repairing the old ones. I guess you might say, "When my work moved up a little, so did my pay!"

Later, I landed a job with a construction contractor to help build the prominent rapid transit system, the Washington Metro. In a support role, I supplied fuel to all of the company's vehicles and heavy equipment, driving a fuel truck around the Washington D.C., area and parts of Northern Virginia. I had to attend to equipment at work sites all over this expansive project, a job that kept me constantly on the move, every day from start to finish. Today this rail system continues to serve thousands of commuter passengers in the capital area and is still one of the largest and busiest rail transit systems in the country.

I played enough years in the big leagues to qualify for the Major League Baseball pension system. Yet, I continued to work at various jobs, aware that the longer I delayed using the plan, the more I would receive for retirement. For that reason, I put in 12 years as a shipyard electrician for the Newport News Shipbuilding Company, servicing and maintaining overhead high-voltage systems that powered the shipyard's gigantic construction cranes. The job involved hard work and long hours, including a long tiring commute. Each week, Monday through Friday I met a bus loaded with shipyard workers which pulled out before sunrise and usually did not return to my neighborhood bus stop until after dark. Keeping those cranes running around the clock was a never ending task which required my department to work lots of extra hours. There were long periods when overtime work was part of our normal schedule, along with weekends and holidays. I frequently had to work seven days a week, which forced me to drive my own private car since the commuter bus schedule wasn't set up to suit my crazy hours. Those were some long, exhausting days. However, those 12 years account for another retirement draw, which now compliments my baseball pension.

Things are much different now. There are days when life is busy and complicated. Yet, I frequently see how it is those days that make life full and rewarding. Often a short pause to smell the roses is all that is needed for me to appreciate what I have. In my small rural community, I never have to look very far to find someone who can use a helping hand. It could be a neighbor or a member of my church, an old friend who is ill or a widow, whose lawn needs mowing. So many who are so near are in need.

I have many things to be thankful for. In particular, I am grateful for the good health I enjoy, for my family and for the many friends I have made along the way. But above all, I am thankful for Dot, my "second-time-around wife," who has given me direction and done so much to keep my life balanced and on track. This lady, who years ago I knew simply as a younger, pesty little girl growing up in the neighborhood, is now the one person who organizes my days and keeps my activities on schedule. Our paths first crossed when she worked as a babysitter, helping Slim and his wife Madeline care for their young daughters, Sandy and Shirley. During an off-season, Dot and I dated a few times after I returned home from baseball. Needless to say, the difference in our ages was a real sticking point, especially for her folks, since Dot had not yet turned fifteen and I was about to start my second season in the minor leagues.

Then our lives went in different directions, with each of us marrying and raising families of our own. Along with being a dedicated wife and mother, she worked locally in the sales division of C&P Telephone which later became part of AT&T, making a career that spanned almost forty years in the communications field. Sometimes she was required to transfer to different offices and even had to relocate her home to suit the demands of the company. Nonetheless, she retired from the business in the fall of 1994 with a perfect attendance record!

It wasn't until after her retirement that Dot left her Florida home and moved back to Virginia. Her intentions at the time were to simply return to her hometown and care for her elderly mother. Yet surprisingly, that was when she came back into my life and changed it forever. Incidentally, it was Dot who insisted that I take a break from my nonstop lifestyle, long enough to collect my thoughts and memories and offer my life story to anyone who will read this book.

Also in 1994, I was humbled when I received word that I had been voted into the Virginia Sports Hall of Fame. My induction placed me in the company of many of the greatest athletes and sports media figures ever to come from my home state. Now, just seeing my name listed with the others on the shrine's roll of honorees is wonderfully gratifying. It was my good friend, Carroll Lee Ashburn who headed the campaign to assure my election. He worked tirelessly, writing letters and making phone calls over a period of several years, until we finally met with success. My sincere appreciation is extended to him and to everyone who endorsed me and lobbied for my induction.

Long ago my sport was baseball. Then years later it was duckpin bowling, to the extent that my brother and I hit the professional circuit. We each won some prize money on the pro tour and collected some hardware for our trophy cases. Duckpin competition developed into another rivalry for the two of us, which continued until the physical demands of the sport eventually caught up with us. So, what is an old former athlete supposed to do? The competitive fires were still burning inside me, along with the fidgety need to keep moving and stay active. For me, my passions turned to the game of golf.

It was in the mid-nineties that the Major League Baseball Players' Alumni Association began to pick up steam and grow as an organization. By that time I was fully retired and I had more opportunities to get involved with the group. As a member for many years, I continue to participate in many of their worthwhile programs. It is a wonderful fraternity that provides former major leaguers with occasions to get together and reminisce about the good old days, while rekindling some old friendships. But more importantly, our primary goal is to raise funds for charities all over the country, as well as for the association itself. Our series of golf tournaments, *Swing with the Legends* is my favorite of all MLBPAA activities. I sign up for these tournaments whenever I can, knowing I will enjoy swinging the clubs again and meeting up with some old buddies. It's great that Dot comes along with me on many of these outings. She seems to enjoy them as much as I do and I can always count on her for support, whenever I take on a charitable cause.

I am mindful of so many gifts God gave me which led me to this point in my life. Because of that, I try to make time for any cause that will benefit anyone who is less fortunate. I strive to help with as many fund raising causes and charitable events as my calendar will allow. I frequently sign autographs to raise money for many benevolent groups, and I plan to continue these efforts for as long as I can. Moreover, I often spend time talking with young ballplayers and working with them to sharpen their skills. In that way I may help a youngster have a chance to advance in baseball and hopefully help him get the kind of opportunities I was given. I believe baseball is still the greatest game in the world, and I will continue to do whatever I can to promote it. From the time I was a young child, baseball was my life's passion and I'm sure it's the same for many kids today.

I have met many famous people in my life and some very unique characters. I have worked at a variety of jobs, including playing baseball for different professional teams, at all levels and in all classifications. Some of these teams were winners while others were not. However, there is one particular organization that leaves its indelible mark on all who pass through its ranks. This elite team embodies history, tradition and pride, and only the best players are chosen to join. I am honored to still be associated with this, the most successful franchise in all of professional sports, the New York Yankees. And though I'll always have wonderful memories of being a part of many different baseball organizations, in my heart, I'll always be a Yankee!

Because God has opened many doors for me throughout my life and blessed me with exceptional talent, I believe now is the time for me to give back as much as I can and show gratitude for all that He has given me.

An occasional vacation trip is another fun part of
life for me and Dot, my "second-time-around" wife.

To benefit a charity or just for fun, today, golf is my game.

Yankee tradition and pride is kept alive by current players like Derek Jeter. I hooked up with him at a recent Yankee reunion.

Old-timers get together: Ralph Terry and I share a few moments on the field with Yankee skipper Joe Torre.

After winning the World Series, some friends from Virginia's Northern Neck honored me with a dinner and gifts. The group included Dr. Tingle and Henry McGinnes.